Elementary Music Theory
Note Speller

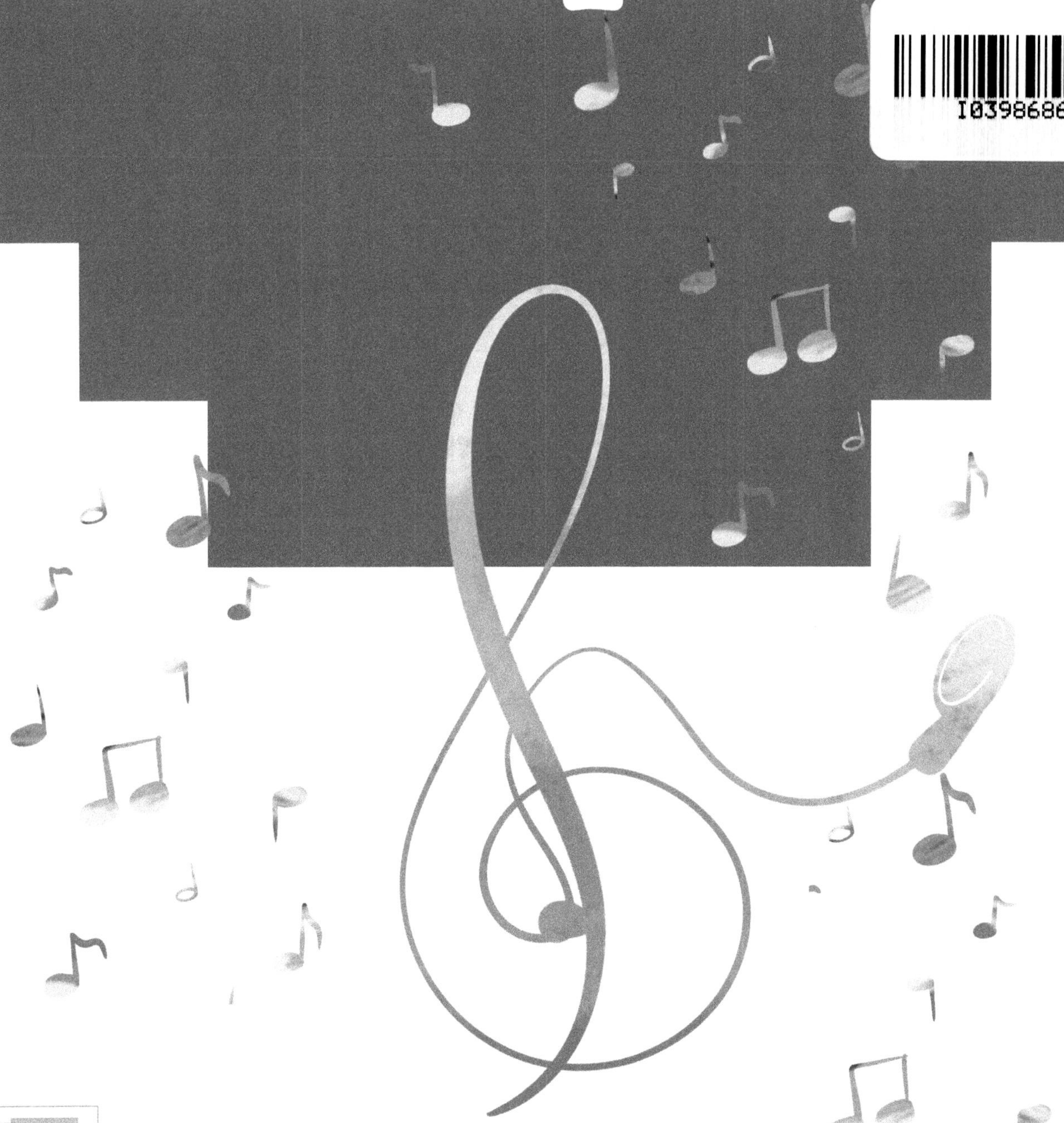

Mark Sarnecki

Elementary Music Theory © 2023 by San Marco Publications. All rights reserved.

All right reserved. No part of this book may be reproduced in any form or by electronic or mechanical means including Information storage and retrieval systems without permission in writing from the author.

ISBN: 9781896499079

Contents

The Treble Staff 2

Spelling Fun 9

Review 1 11

The Bass Staff 14

Spelling Fun 21

Review 2 23

Notes on Ledger Lines 26

The Grand Staff 29

Review 3 33

The Treble Staff

Music is written on five lines and in four spaces called the **staff**.

Higher pitched notes are written in the **treble clef**.

The treble clef is placed and the beginning of the staff.

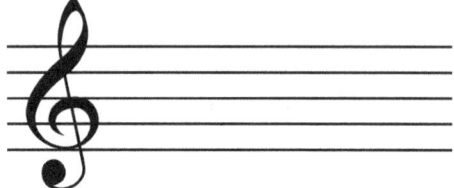

This is how you draw a treble clef!

Trace these treble clefs.

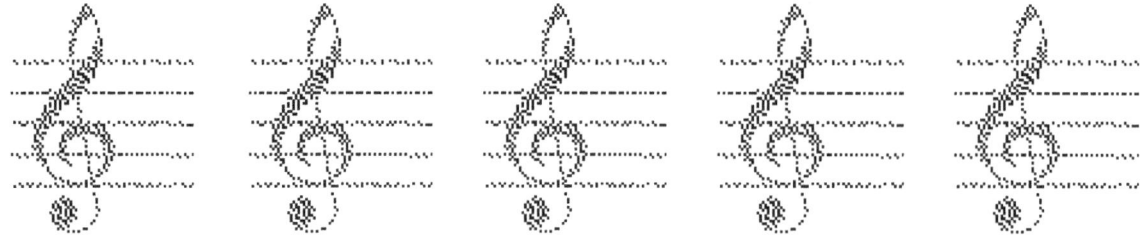

Draw treble clefs in the spaces below.

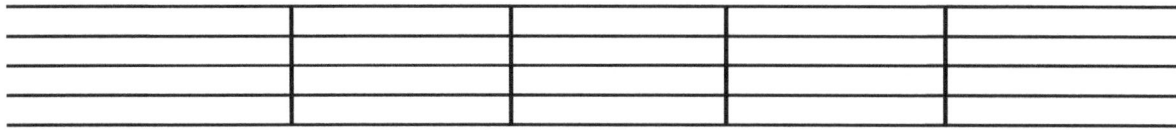

Notes in Spaces in the Treble Clef

The notes in the four spaces on the treble staff spell the word **F A C E**.

Copy this example eight times. Name each note.

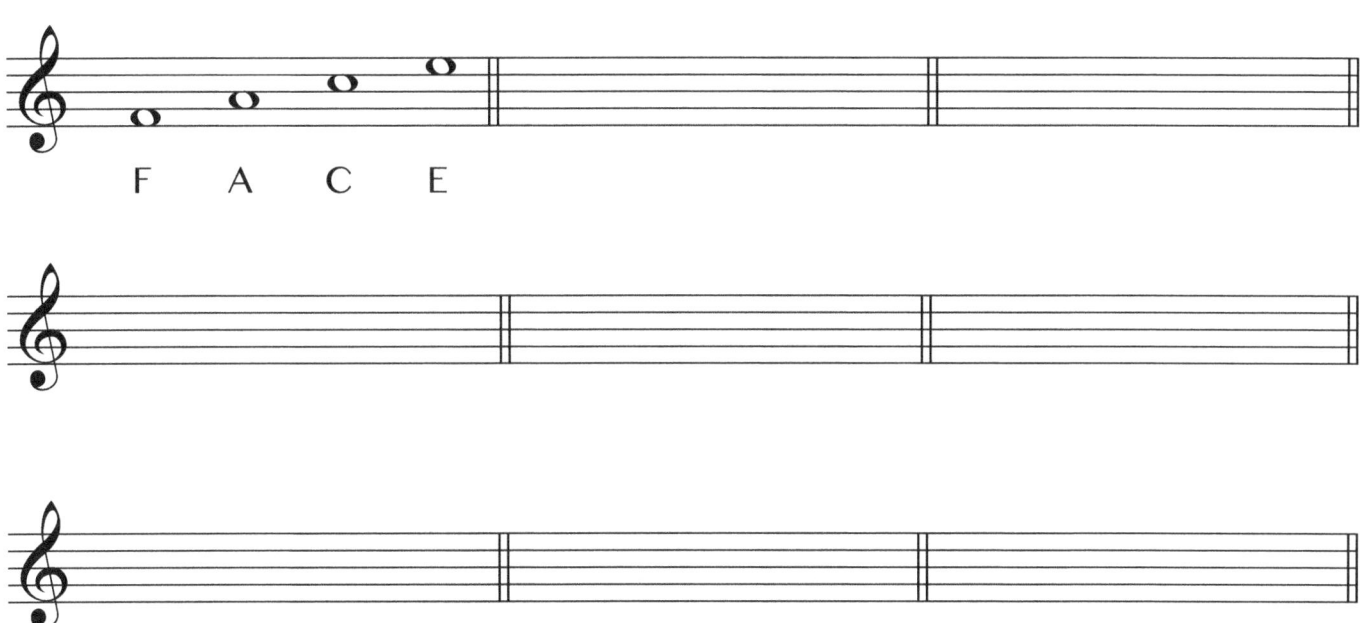

Name the following notes.

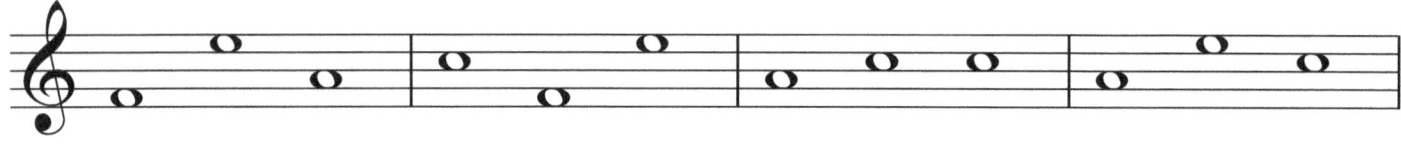
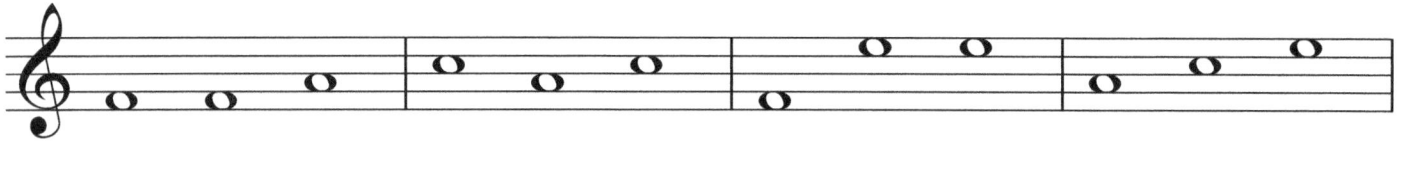
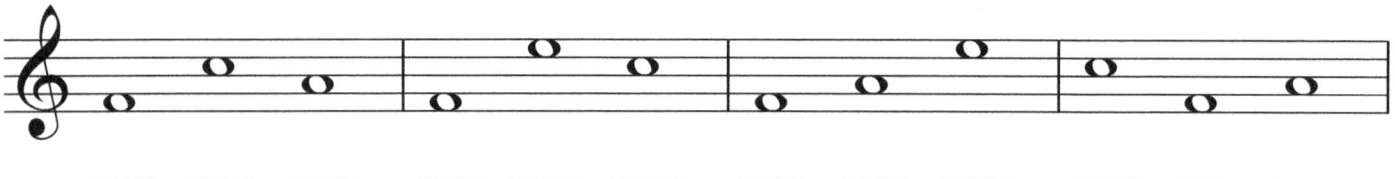
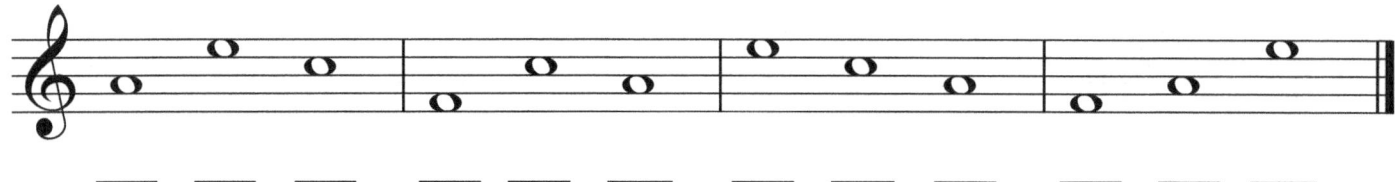

Write the following notes in **spaces**.

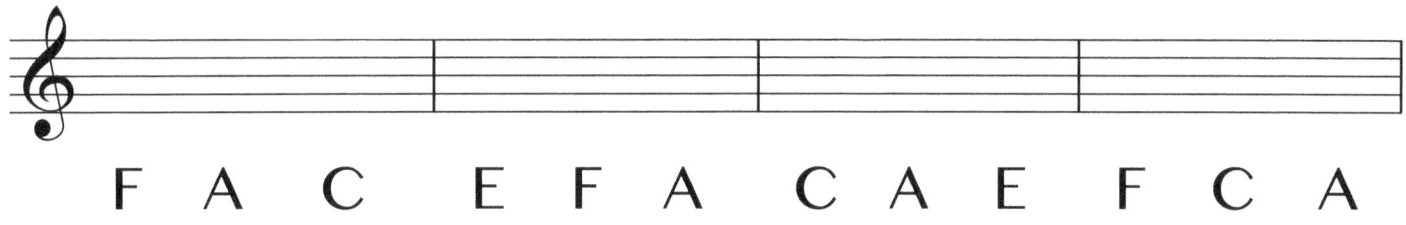

F A C   E F A   C A E   F C A

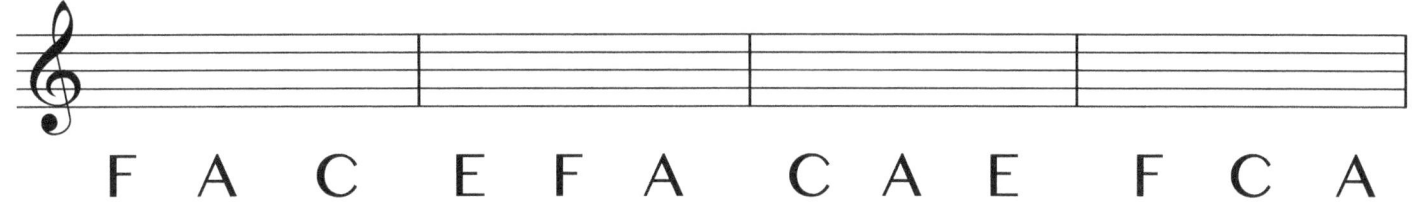

F A C   E F A   C A E   F C A

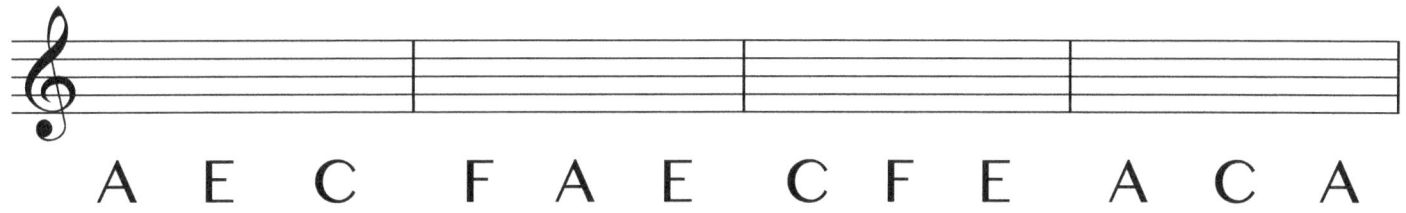

A E C   F A E   C F E   A C A

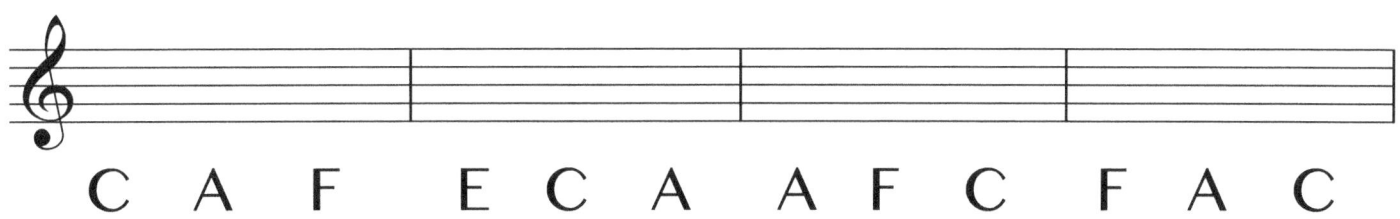

C A F   E C A   A F C   F A C

A E A   F A C   E A E   A C F

Notes on Lines in the Treble Clef

The notes on the five lines of the treble staff are **E G B D F**.

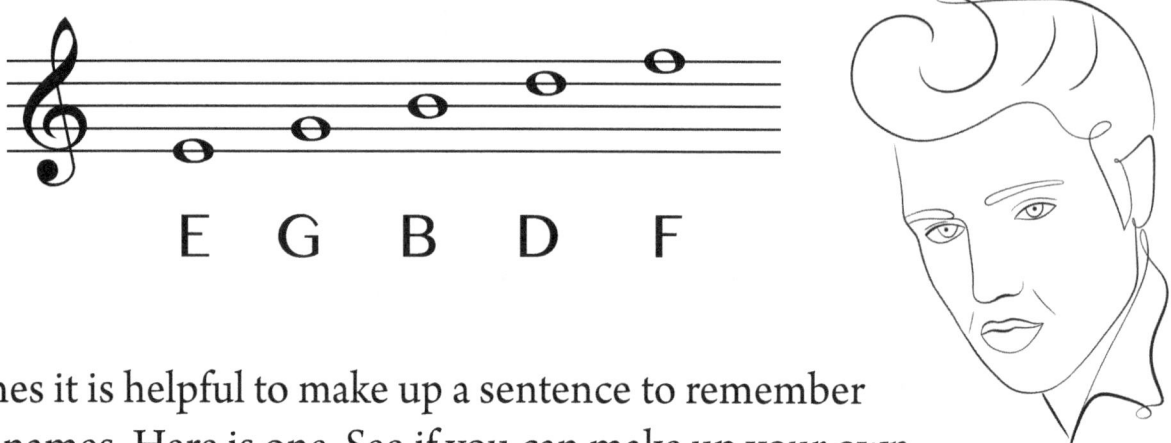

Sometimes it is helpful to make up a sentence to remember the note names. Here is one. See if you can make up your own.

Elvis' **G**uitar **B**roke **D**own **F**riday

Copy this example eight times. Name each note.

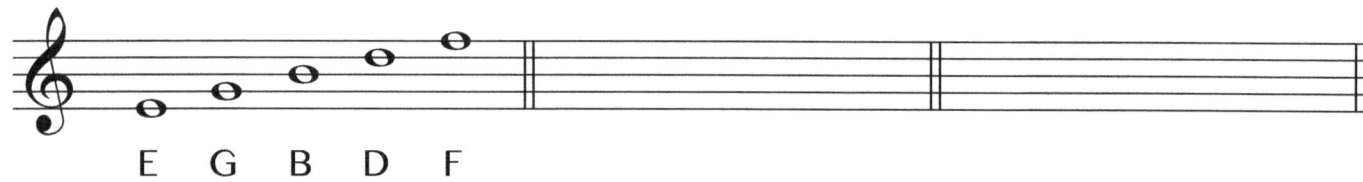

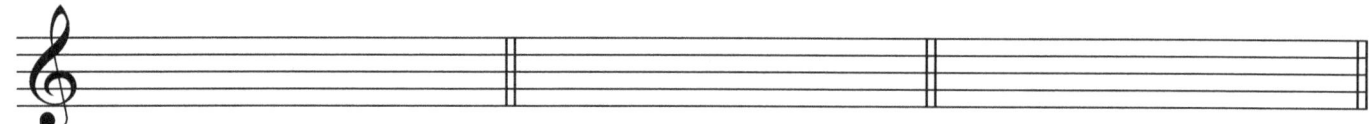

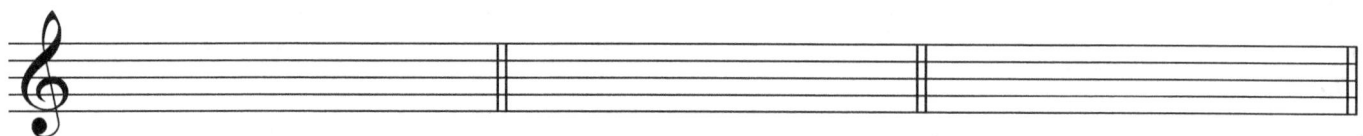

Name the following notes.

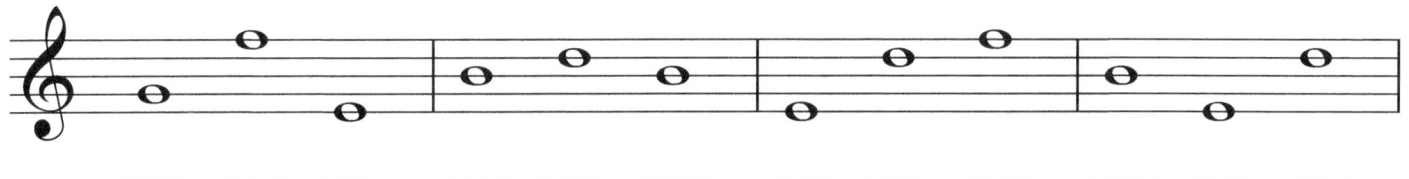

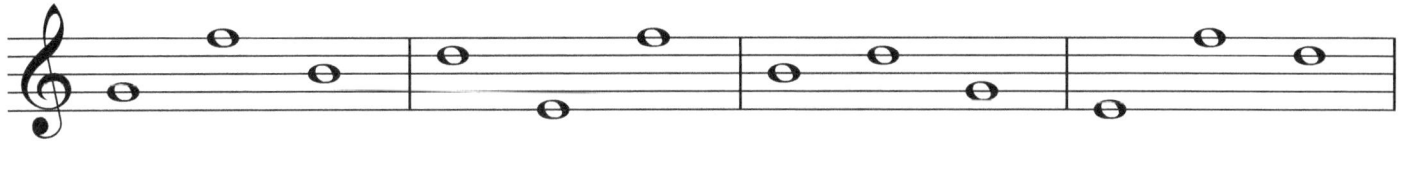

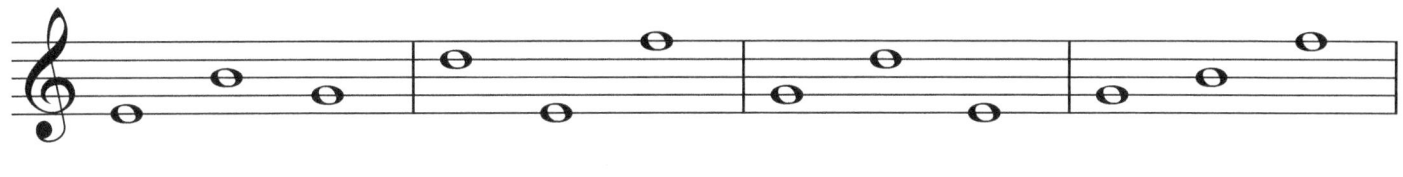

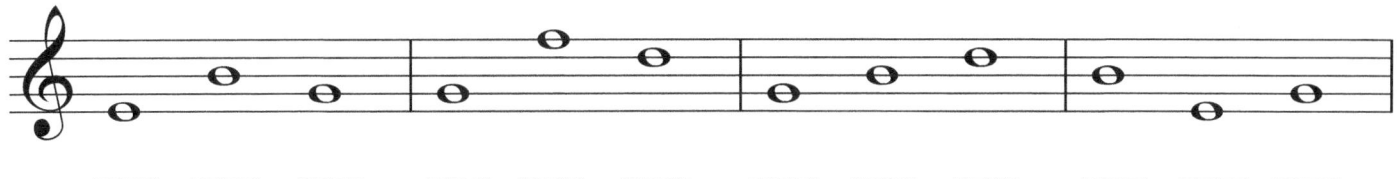

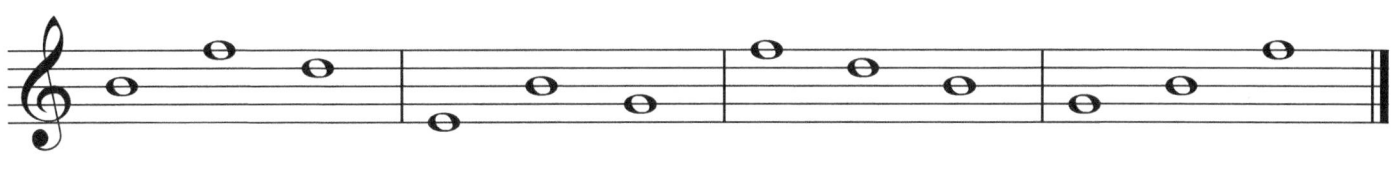

Write the following notes on **lines**.

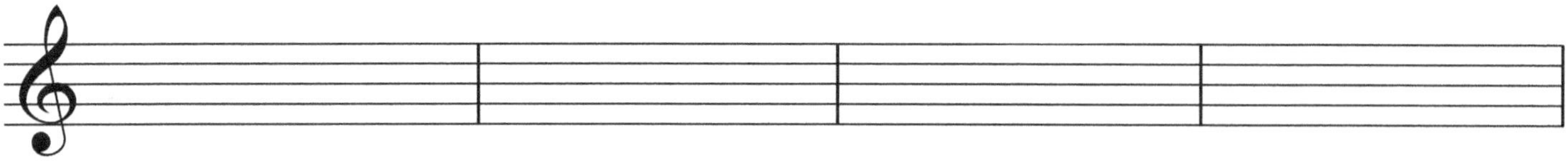

E G B   D F G   D E B   G D F

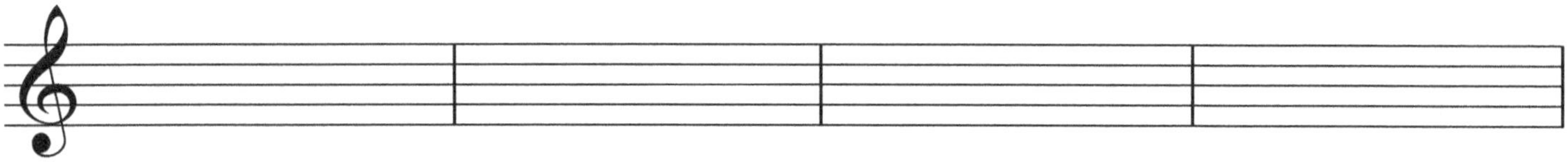

F E D   E G B   G D E   F G B

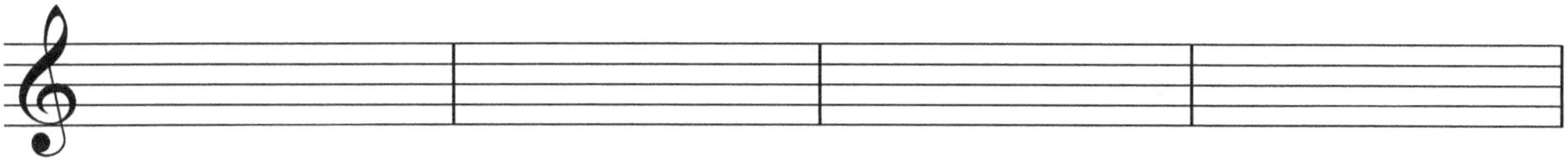

D E G   F B E   D F B   G D B

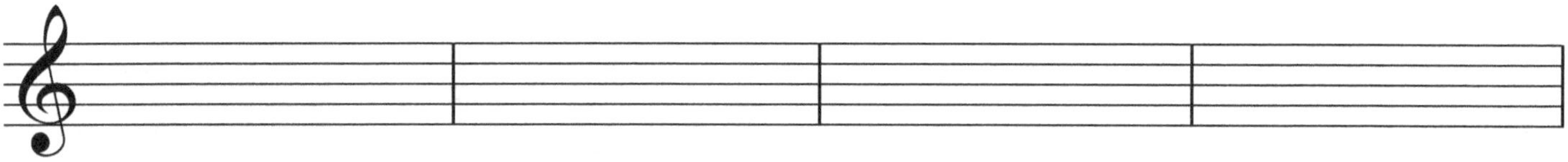

D B F   E G D   B F E   F D G

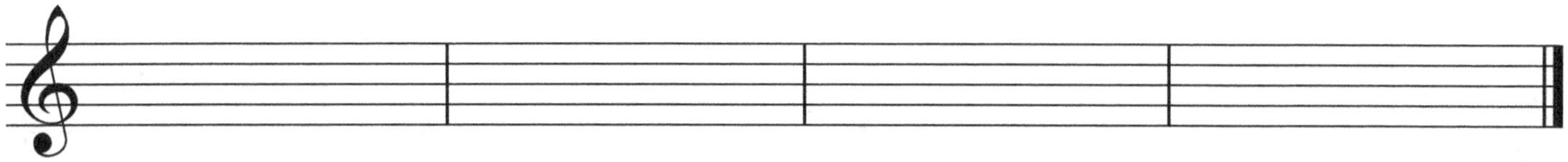

D E G   F B D   E F D   G B F

Spelling Fun

Name the following notes which spell words.

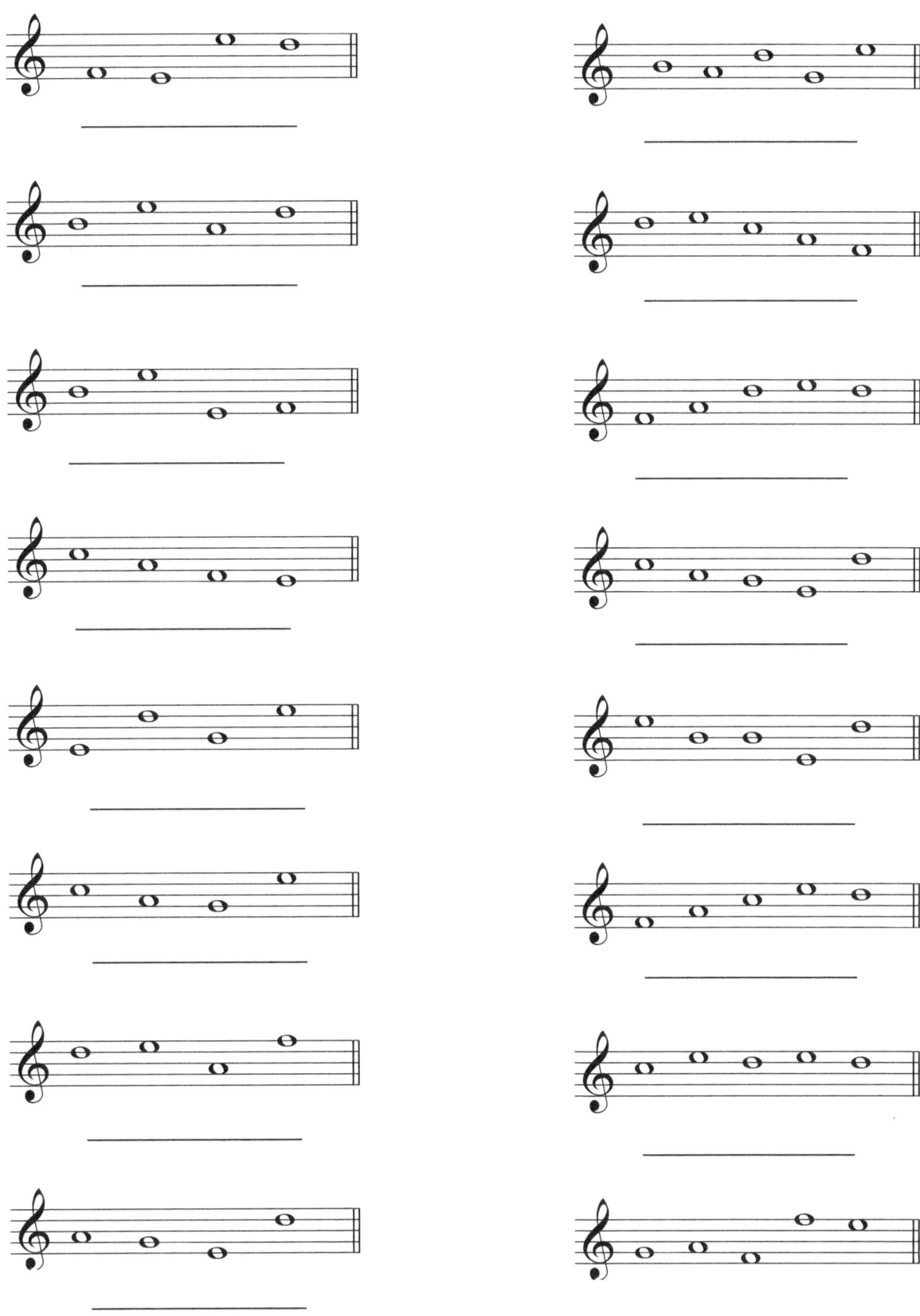

Write the following words using notes on the treble staff.

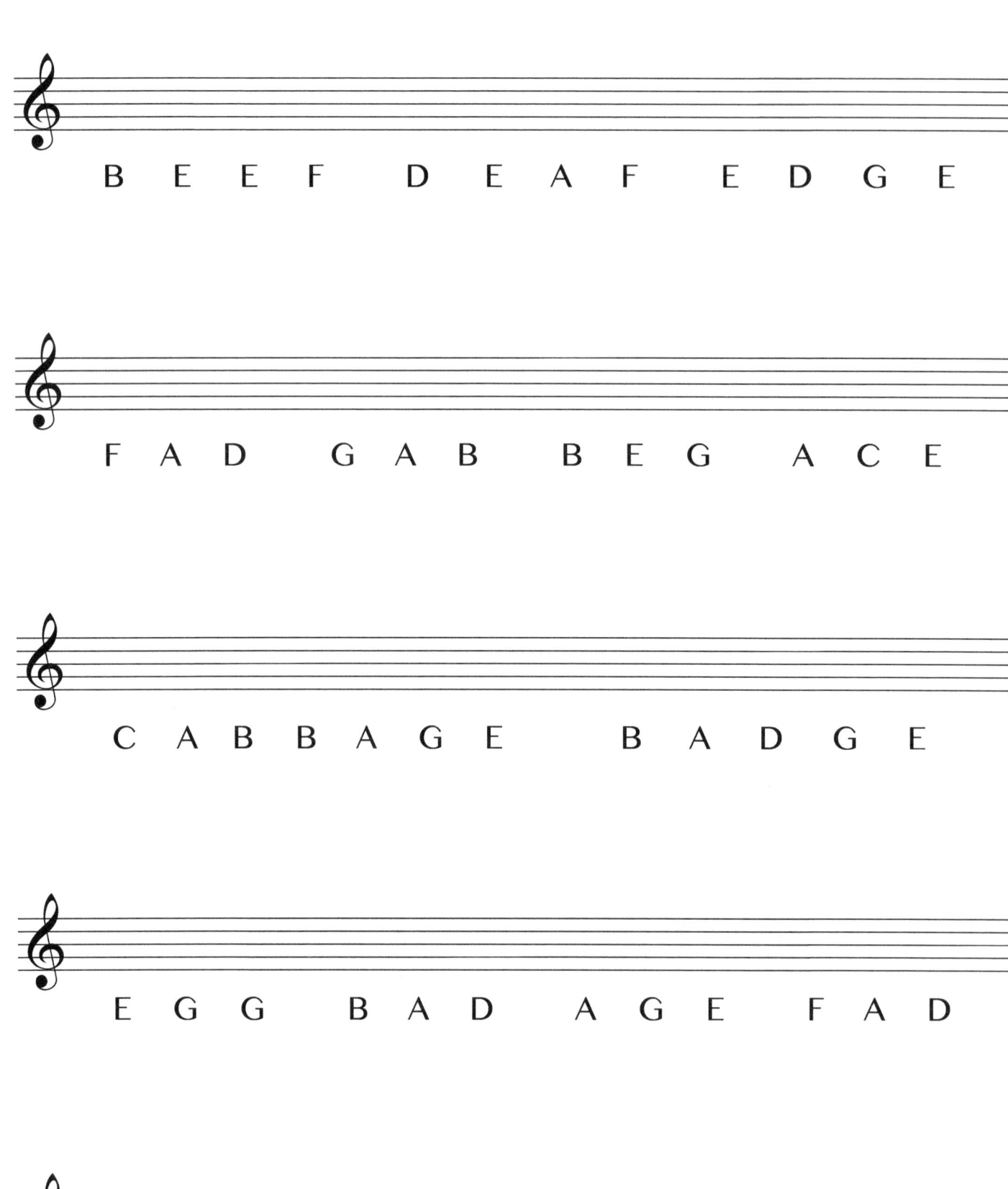

Review 1

1. The higher notes in music are written on the _____ staff.

2. The notes of the five lines on the treble staff are: ___ ___ ___ ___ ___ .

3. The notes in the four spaces of the treble staff are: ___ ___ ___ ___ .

4. Draw five treble clefs.

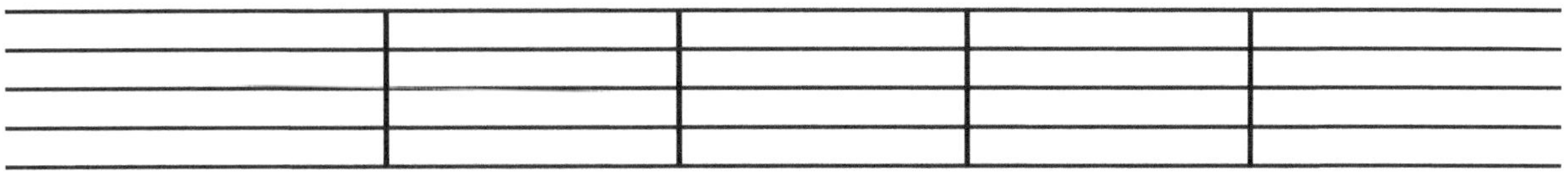

5. Write and name the notes in the spaces of the treble staff.

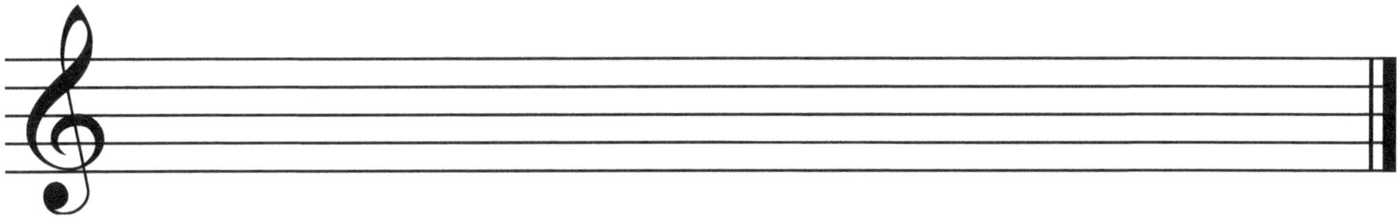

6. Write and name the notes on the lines of the treble staff.

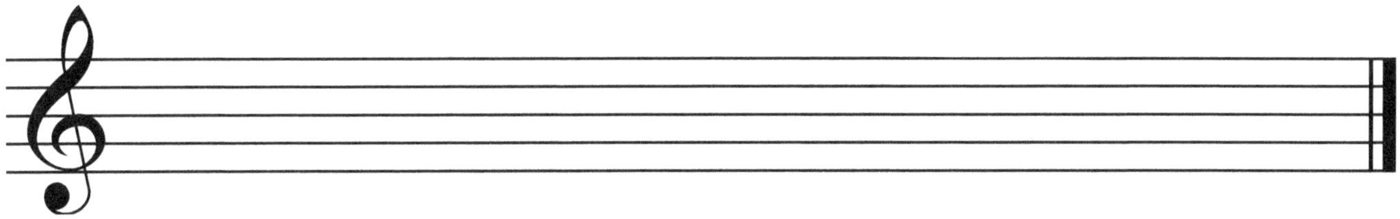

7. Name the following notes.

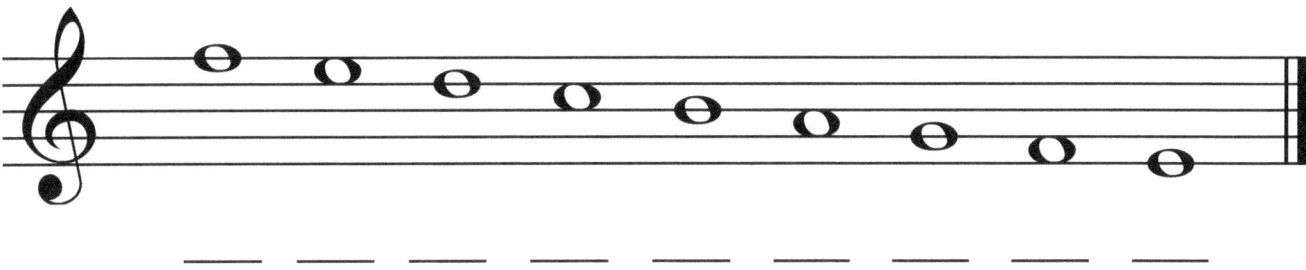

8. Name the following notes.

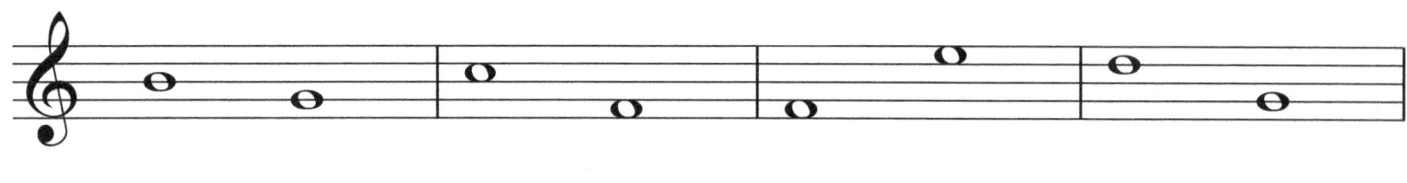

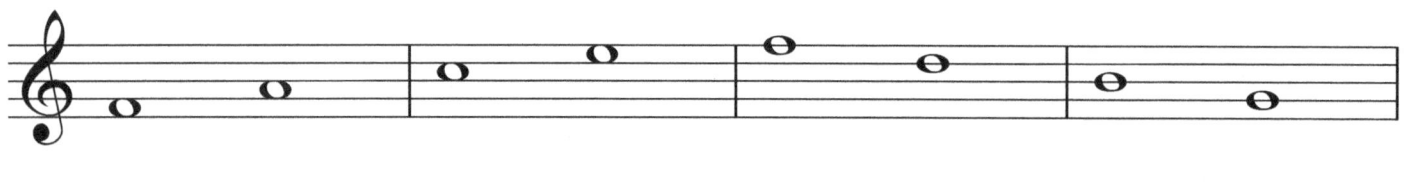

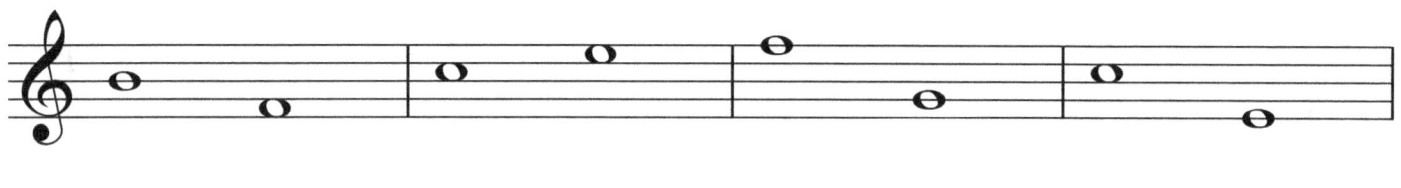

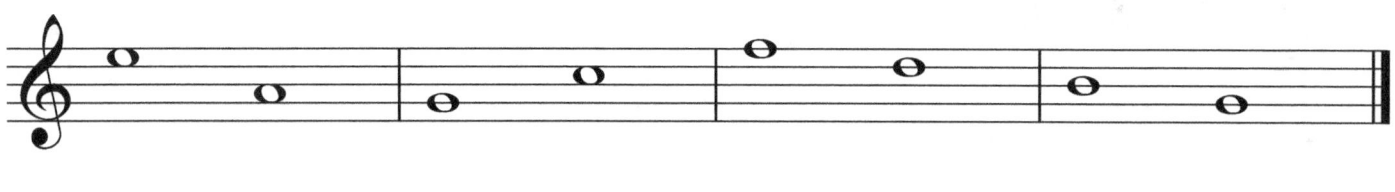

9. Write the following notes.

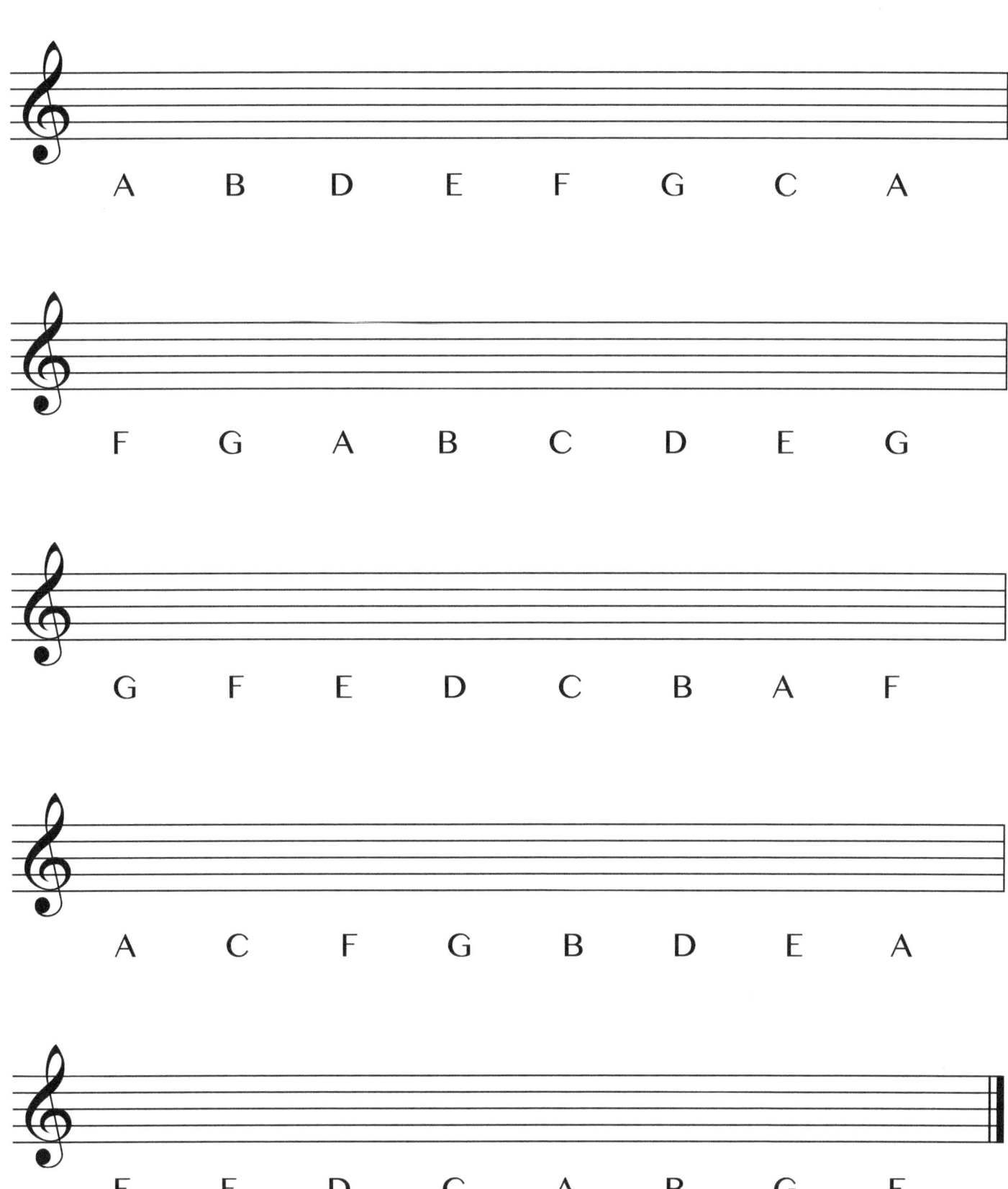

The Bass Staff

Lower pitched notes are written on the **bass staff**.

On the keyboard the left hand usually plays in the bass staff.

The **bass clef** is placed and the beginning of the staff.

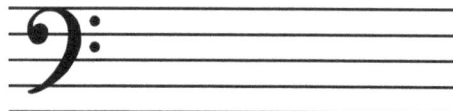

This is how you draw a bass clef!

1. 2. 3.

Trace these bass clefs.

   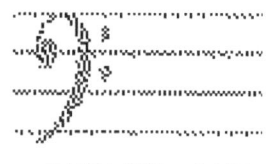

Draw bass clefs in the spaces below.

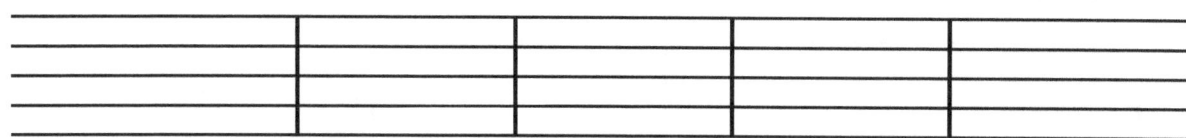

Notes in Spaces in the Bass Clef

The notes in the spaces on the bass staff are: A C E G.

Copy this example eight times. Name each note.

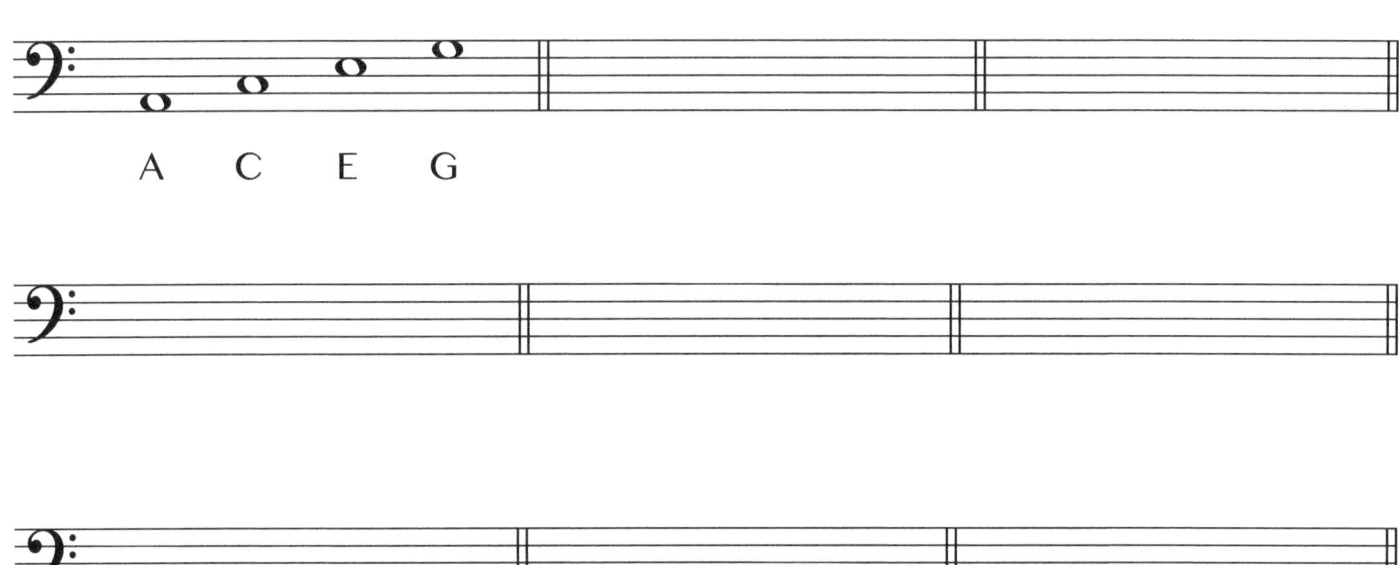

Name the following notes.

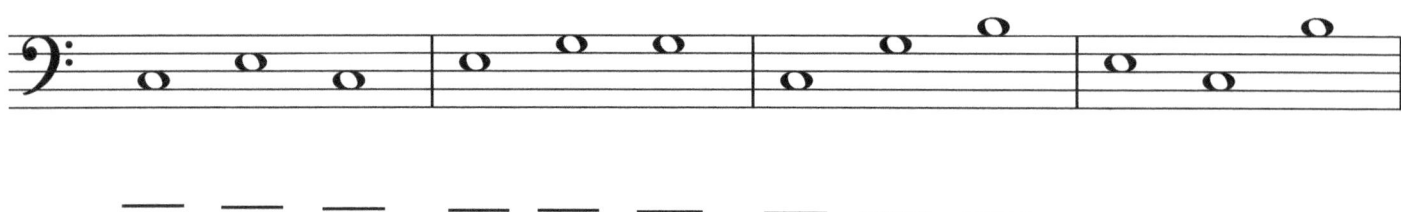

_ _ _   _ _ _   _ _ _   _ _ _

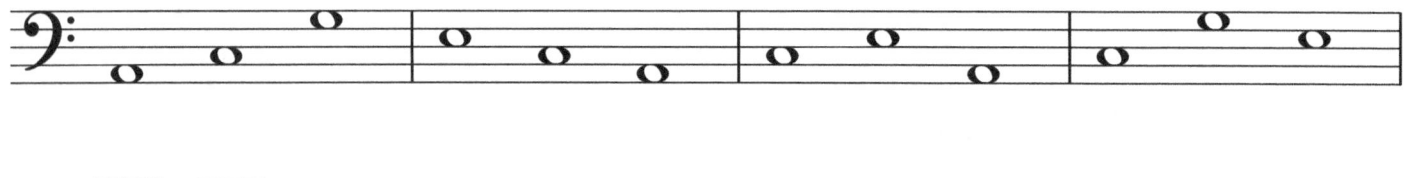

_ _ _   _ _ _   _ _ _   _ _ _

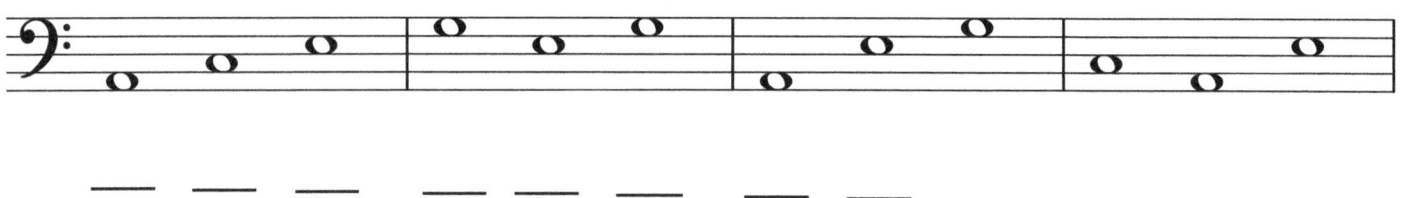

_ _ _   _ _ _   _ _ _   _ _ _

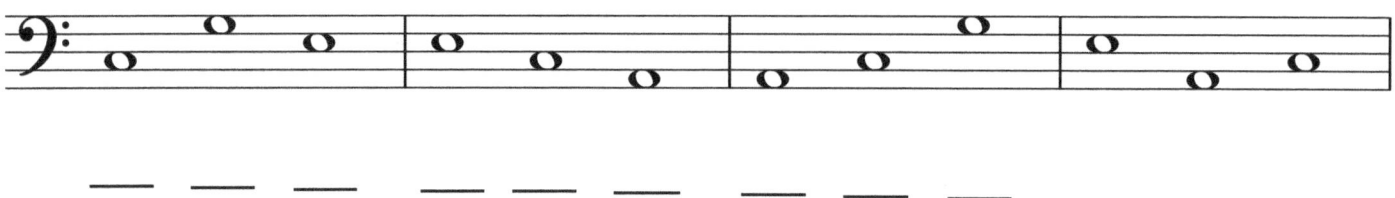

_ _ _   _ _ _   _ _ _   _ _ _

_ _ _   _ _ _   _ _ _   _ _ _

Write the following notes in **spaces**.

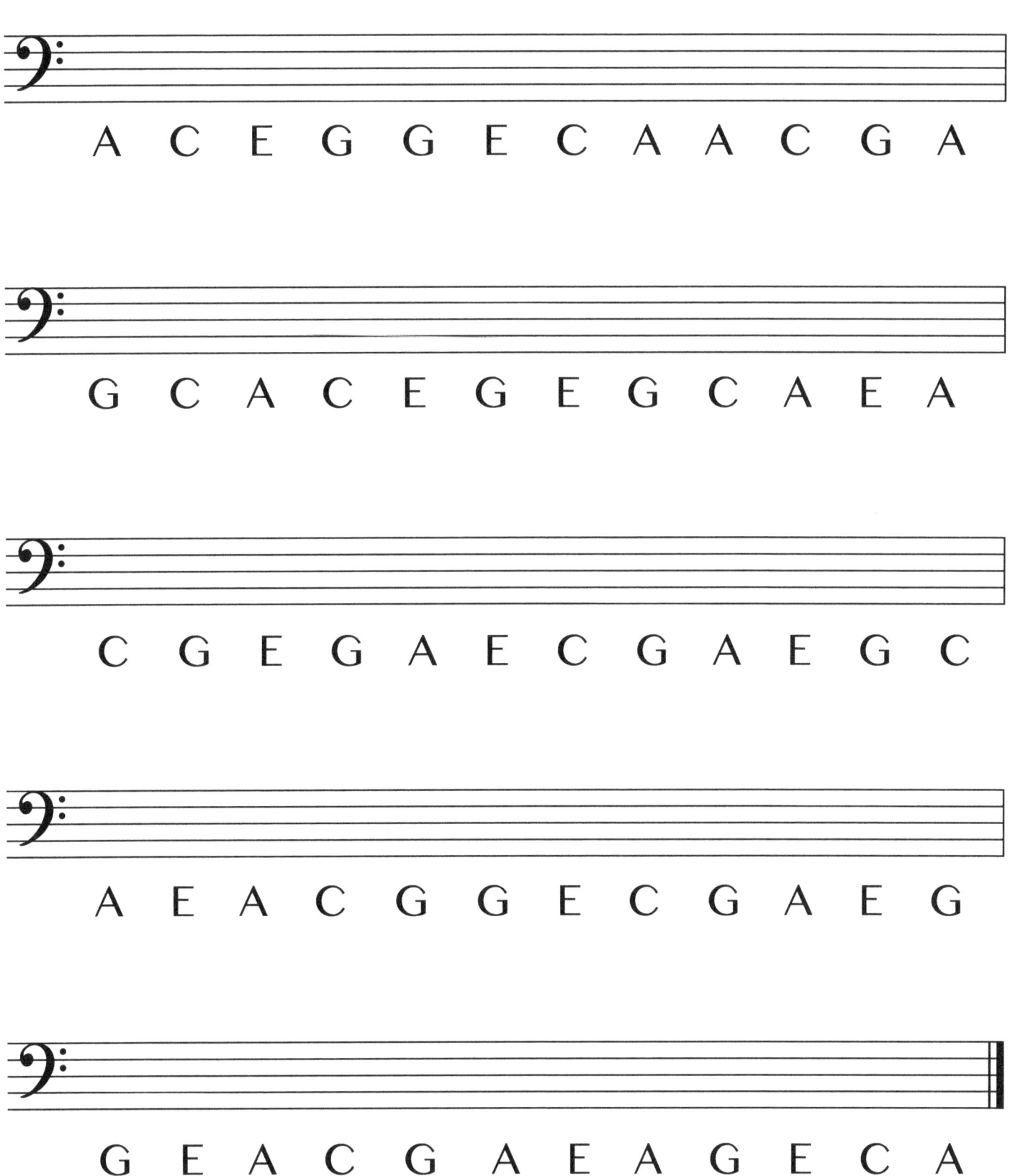

Notes on Lines in the Bass Clef

The notes on the 5 lines of the bass staff are: G B D F A.

Copy this example eight times. Name each note.

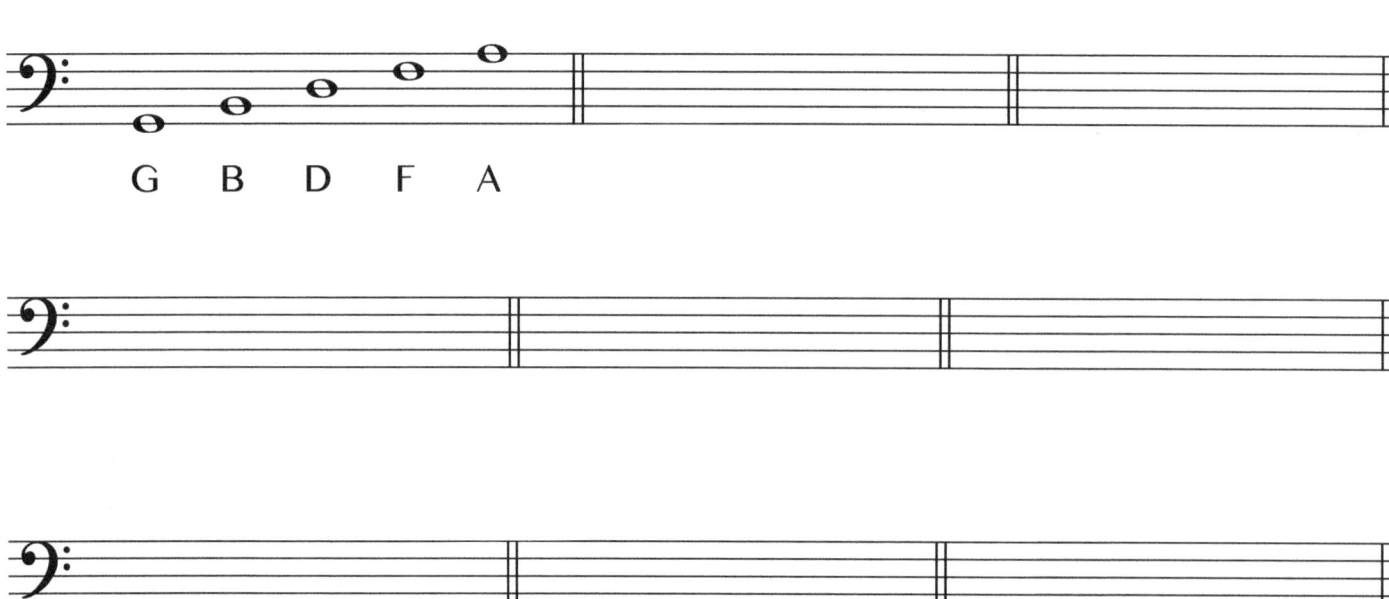

Name the following notes.

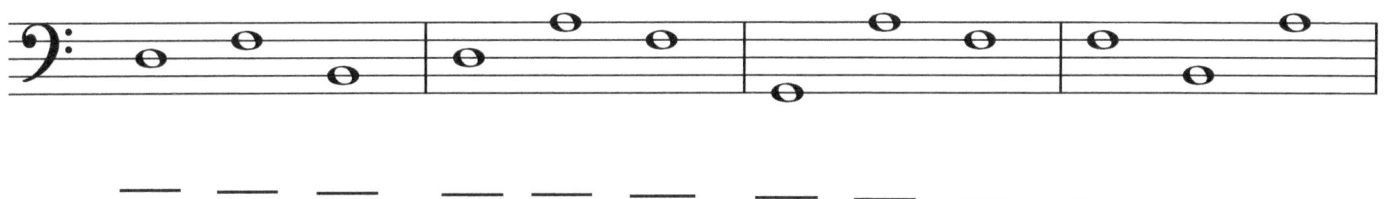

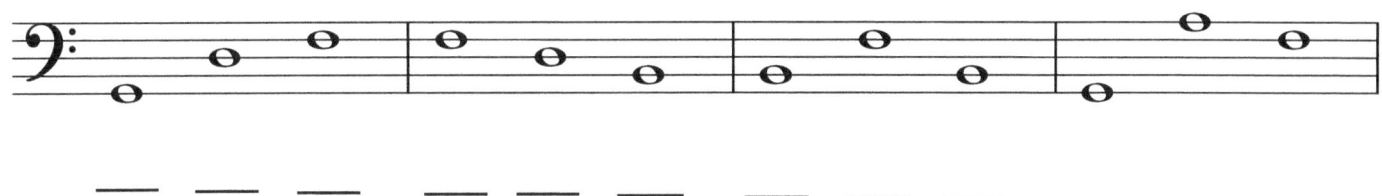

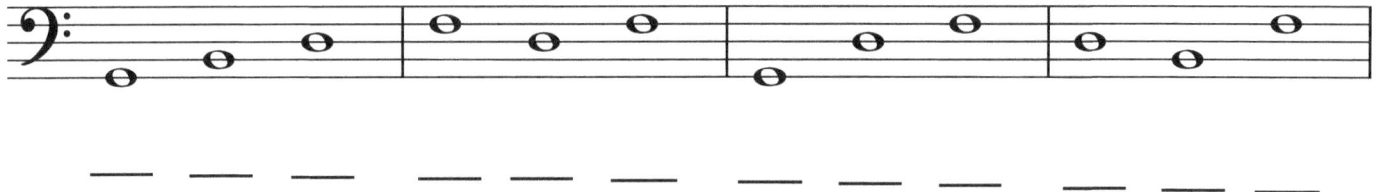

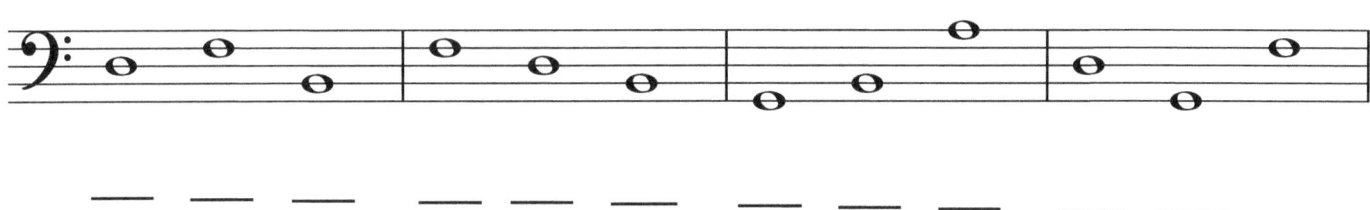

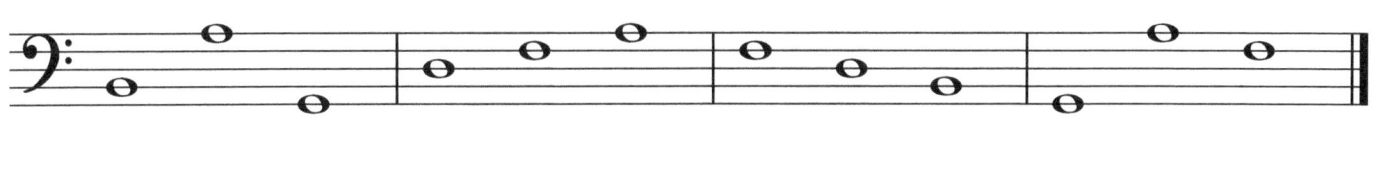

Write the following notes in **lines.**

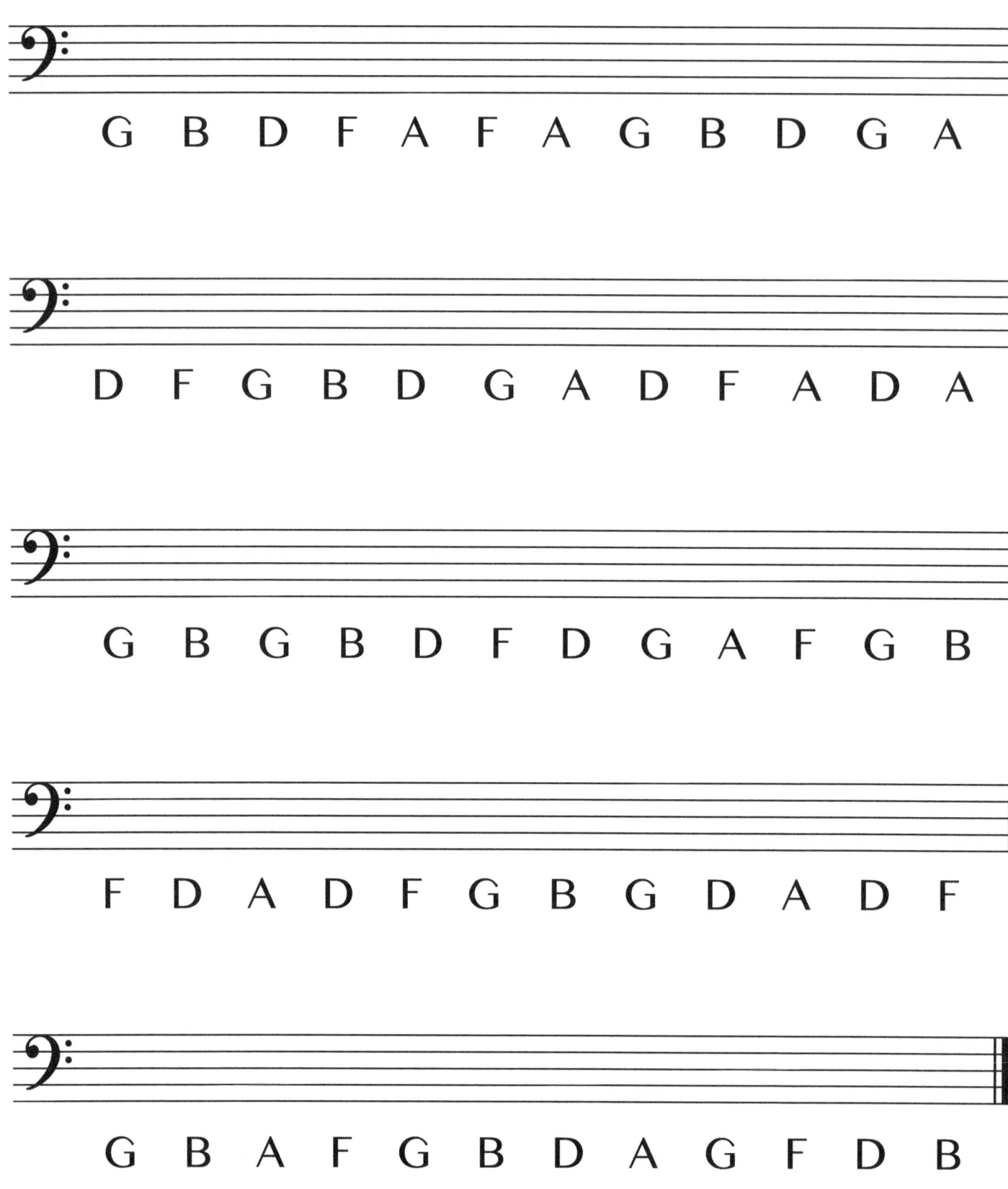

Spelling Fun

Name the following notes which spell words.

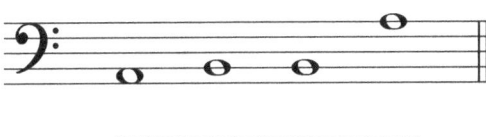
_____

_____

_____

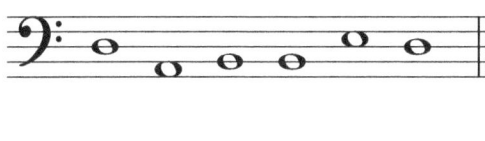
_____

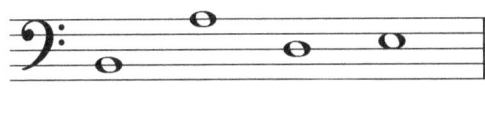
_____

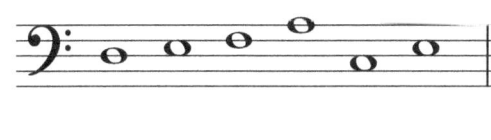
_____

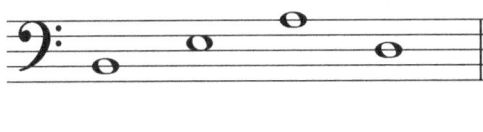
_____

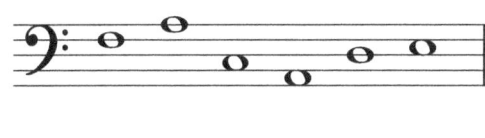
_____

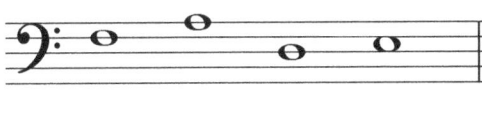
_____

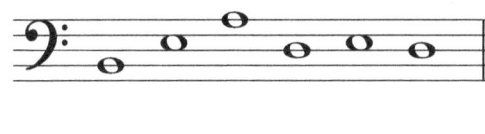
_____

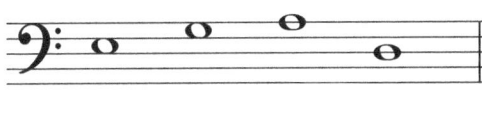
_____

_____

Write the following words using notes on the bass staff.

𝄢

BADGE   BAGGAGE

𝄢

BEE   AGE   BAD   EGG

𝄢

FACE   GAGE   BEEF

𝄢

DECADE   BEADED

𝄢

FEEDBAG   BABA

Review 2

1. The lower notes in music are written on the _____ staff.

2. The notes of the five lines on the bass staff are: ___ ___ ___ ___ ___ .

3. The notes in the four spaces of the bass staff are: ___ ___ ___ ___ .

4. Draw five bass clefs.

5. Write and name the notes in the spaces of the treble staff.

6. Write and name the notes on the lines of the treble staff.

7. Name the following notes.

___ ___ ___ ___ ___ ___ ___ ___ ___

8. Name the following notes.

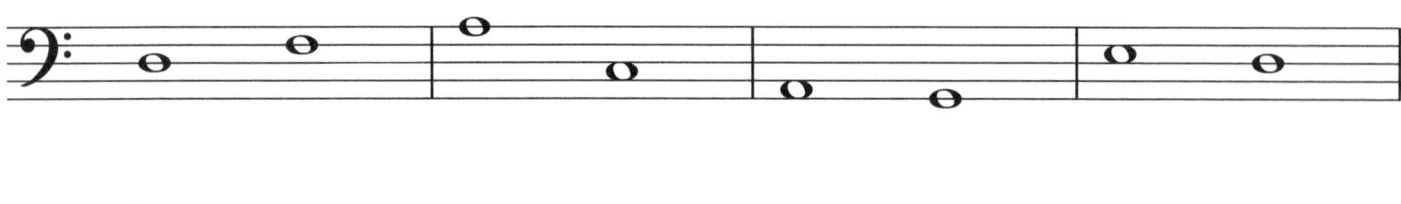

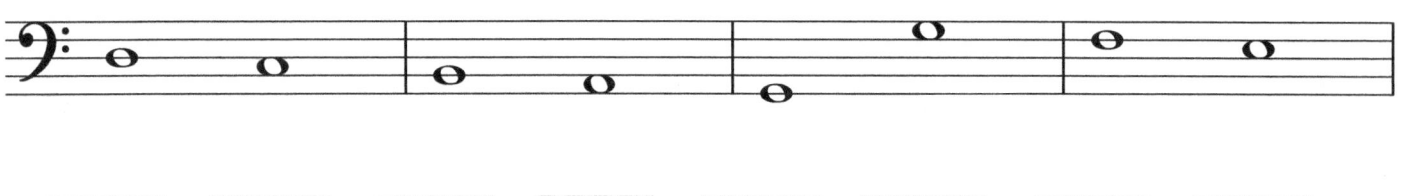

9. Write the following notes.

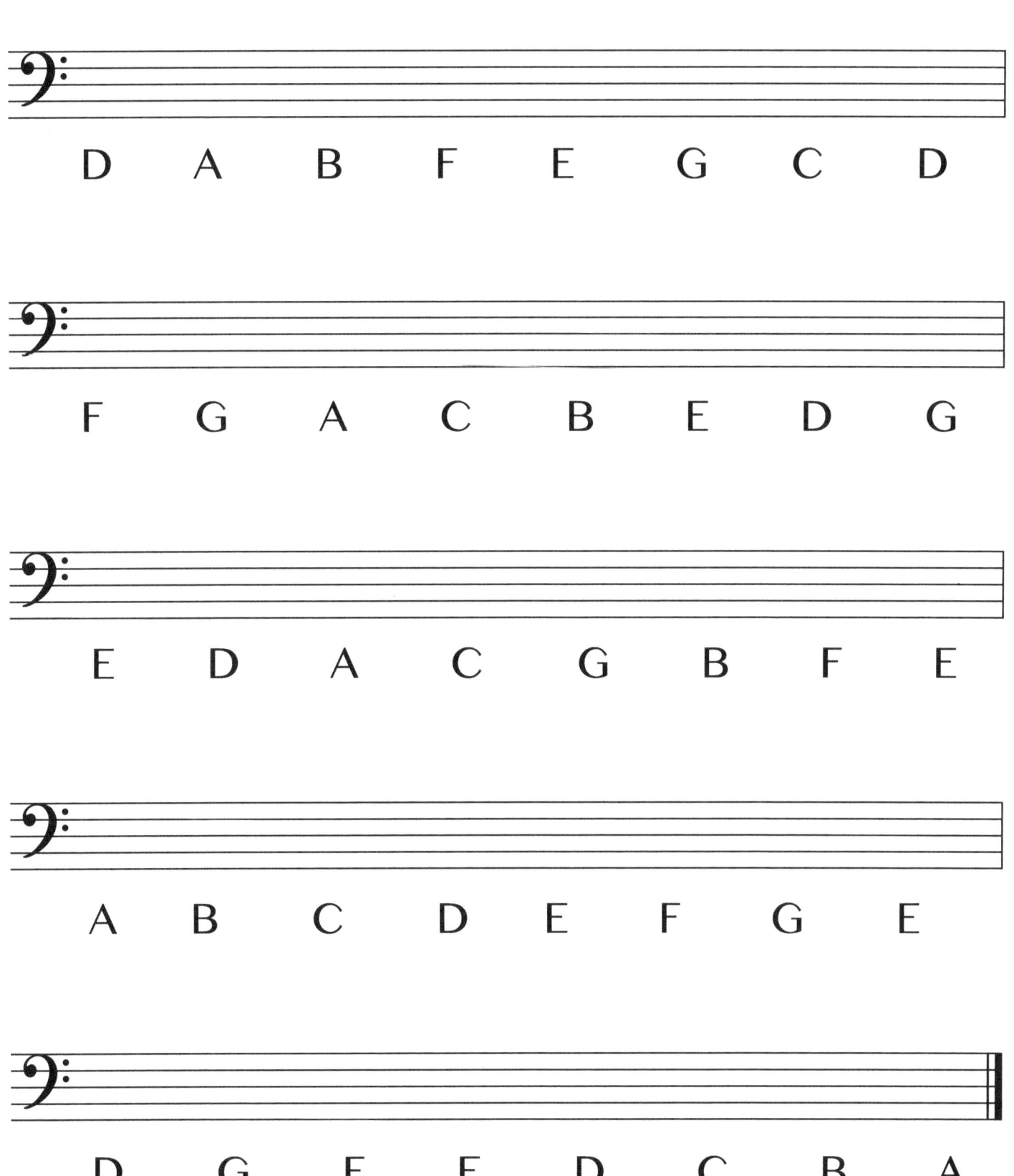

Notes on Ledger Lines: The Treble Staff

We use small lines called **ledger lines** to extend the range of the staff. These lines are used for notes that are above or below the five lines and four spaces of the staff.

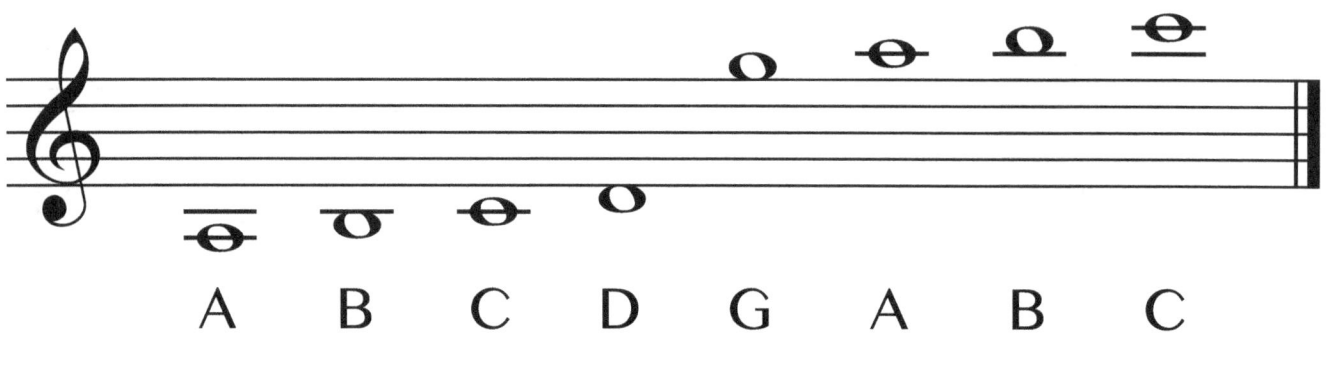

Name the following notes.

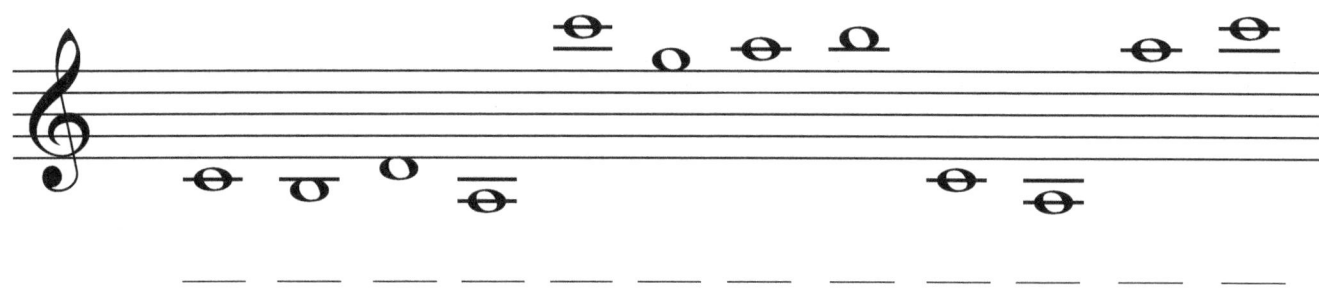

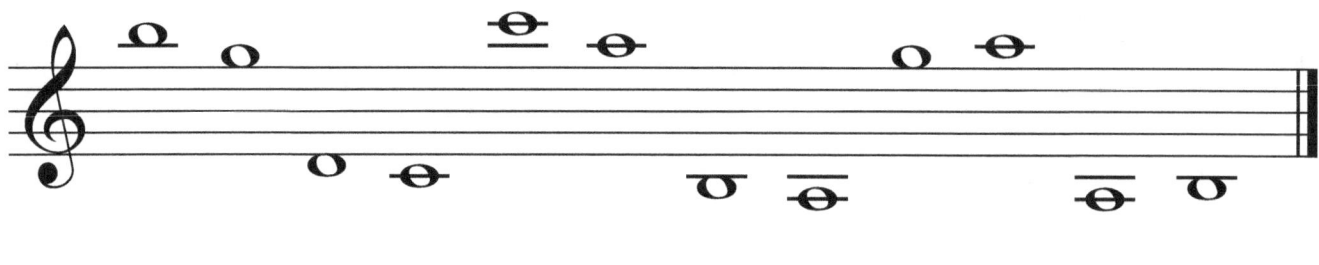

Notes on Ledger Lines: The Bass Staff

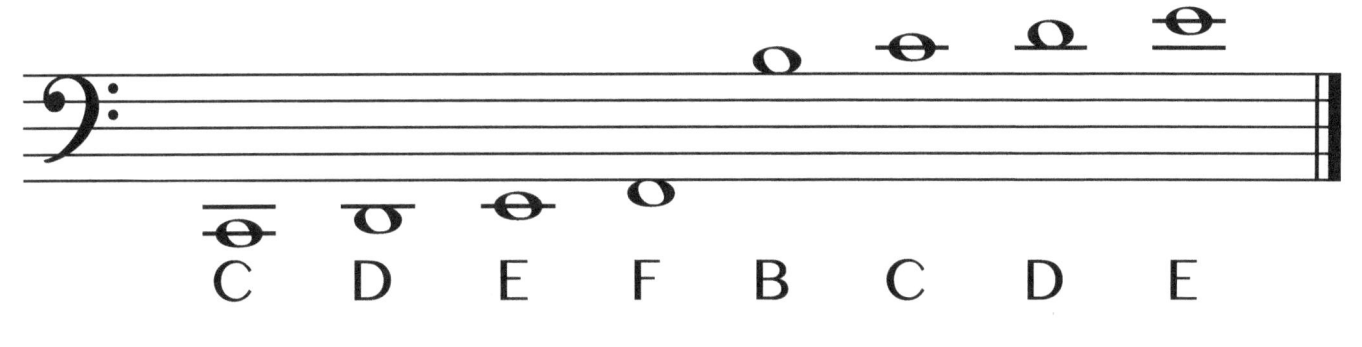

Name the following notes.

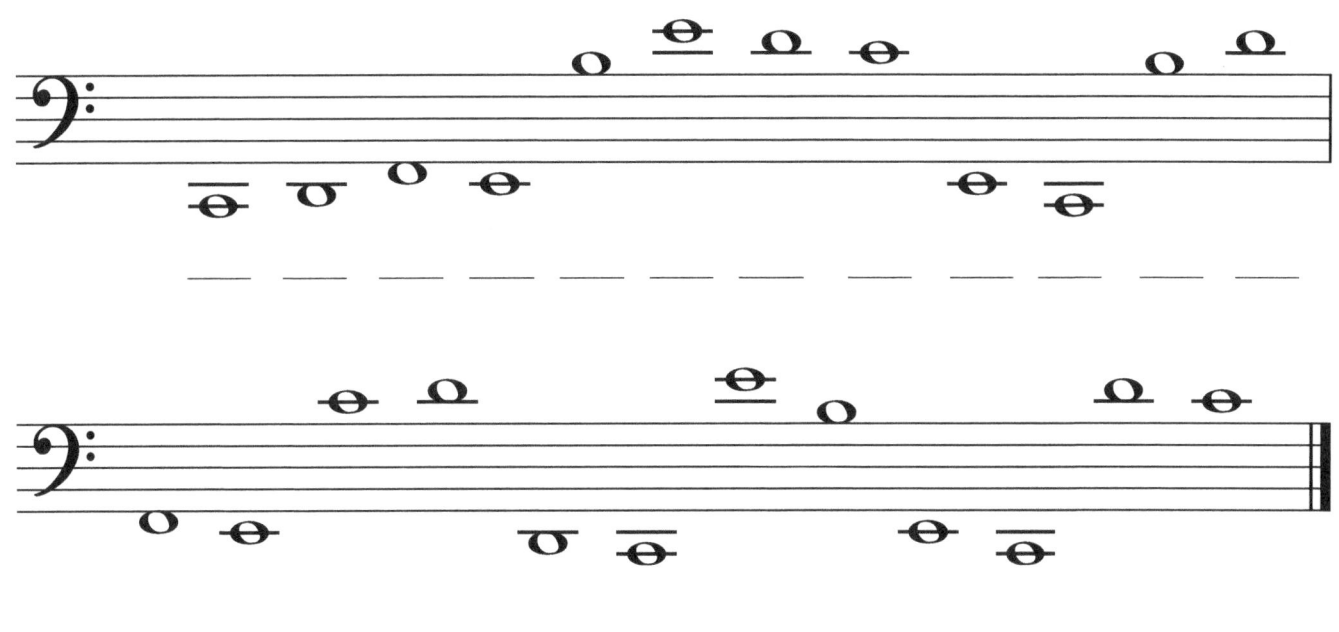

Write the following ledger line notes.

Name the following notes.

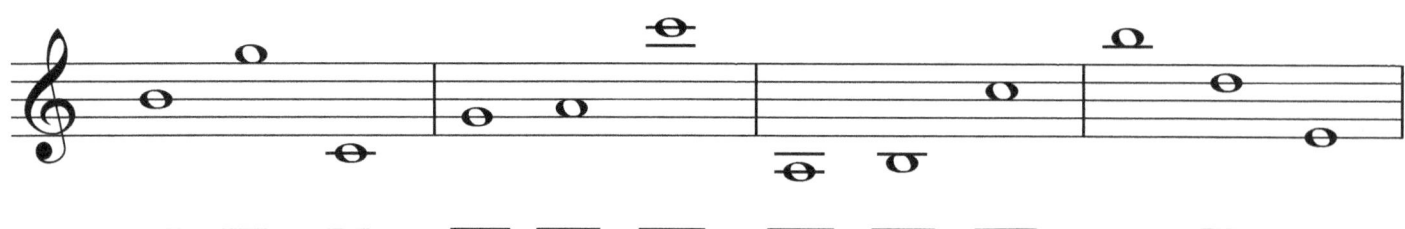

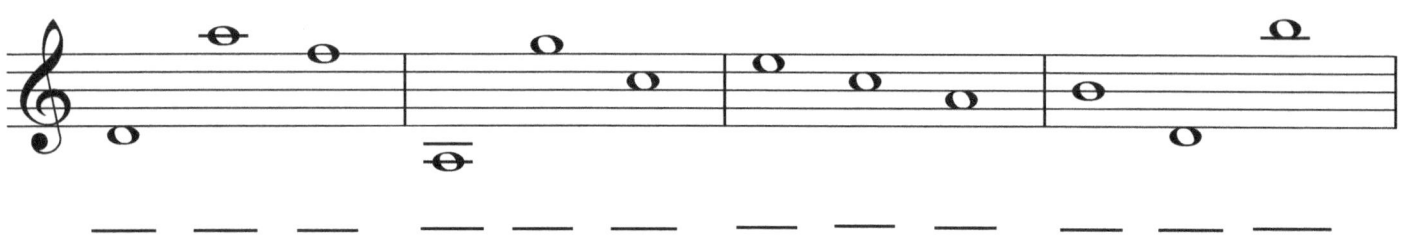

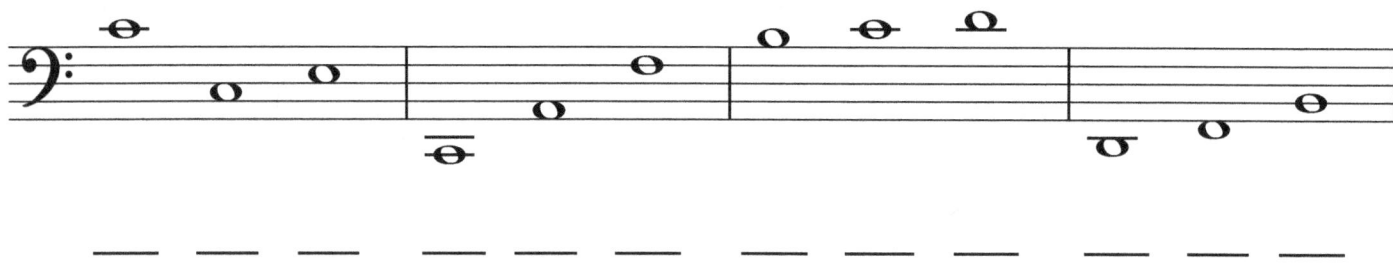

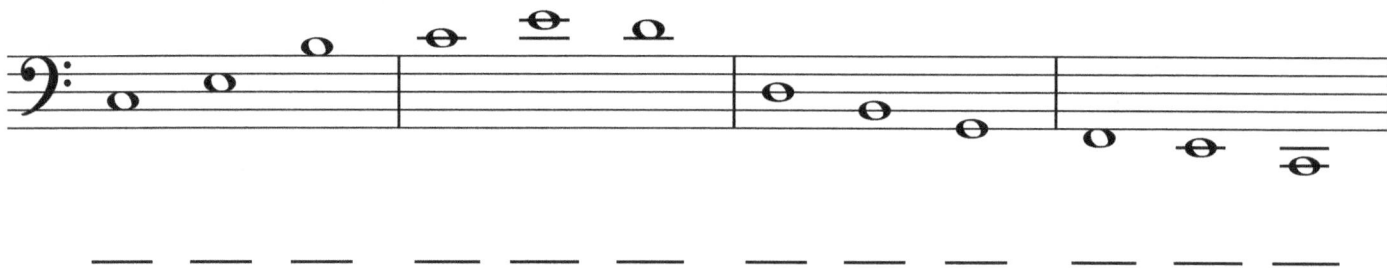

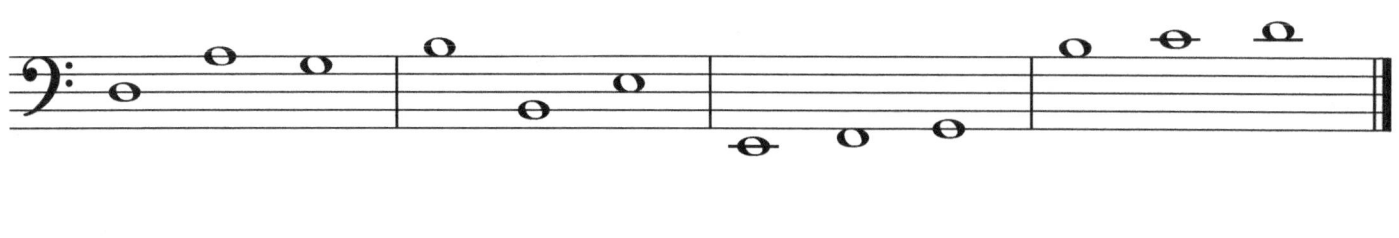

The Grand Staff

The treble and bass staves are combined to make the **grand staff**.

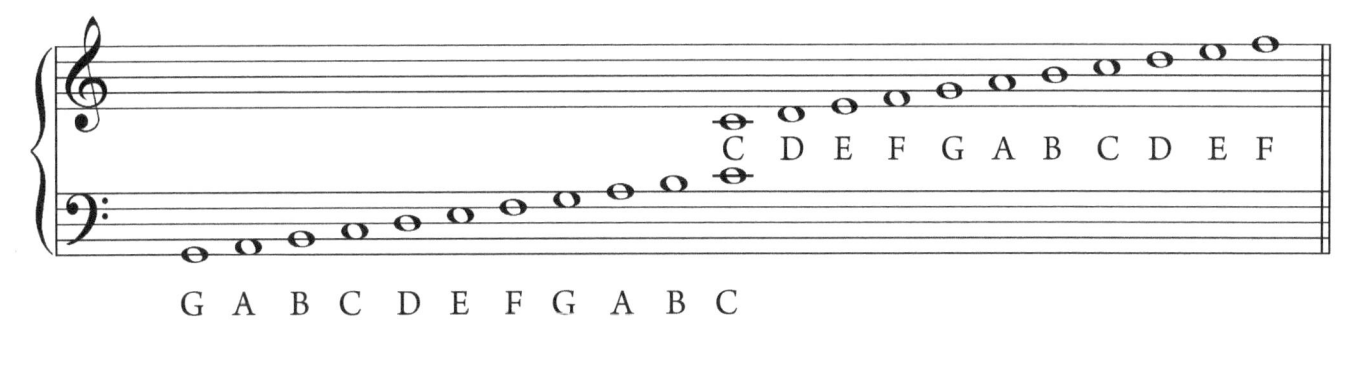

Write all the notes in the grand staff twice. Name each note.

Name the following notes.

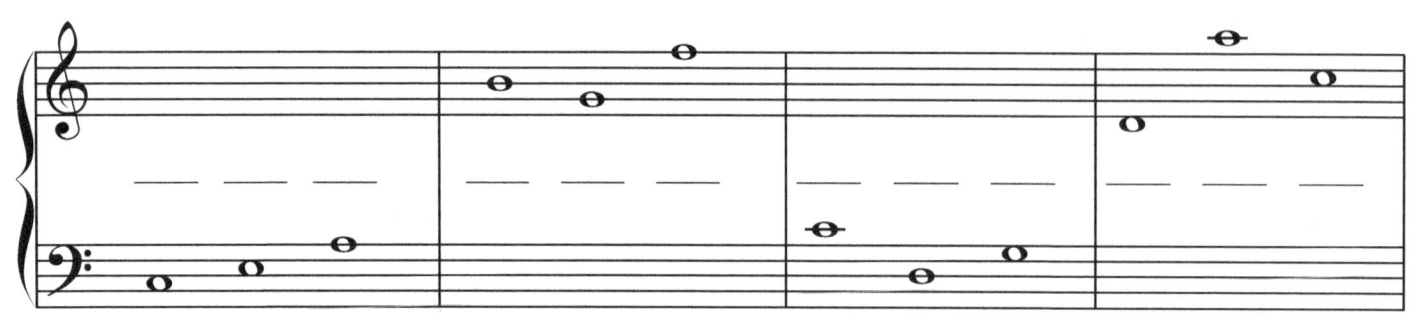
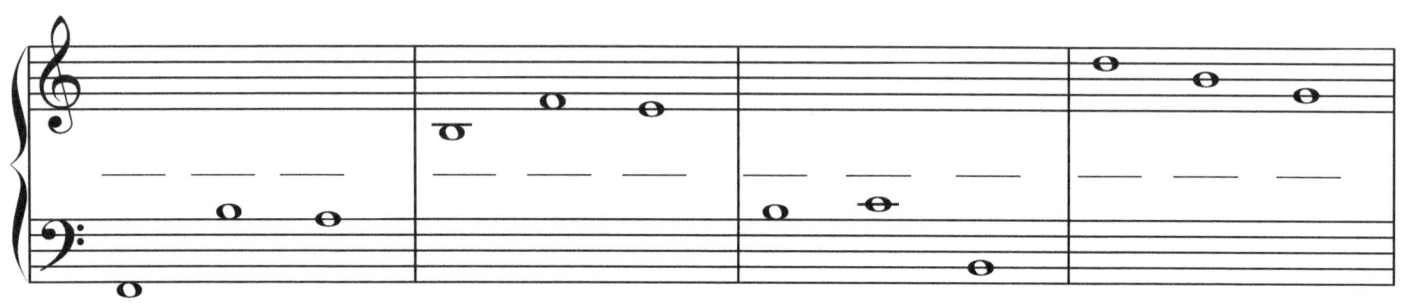
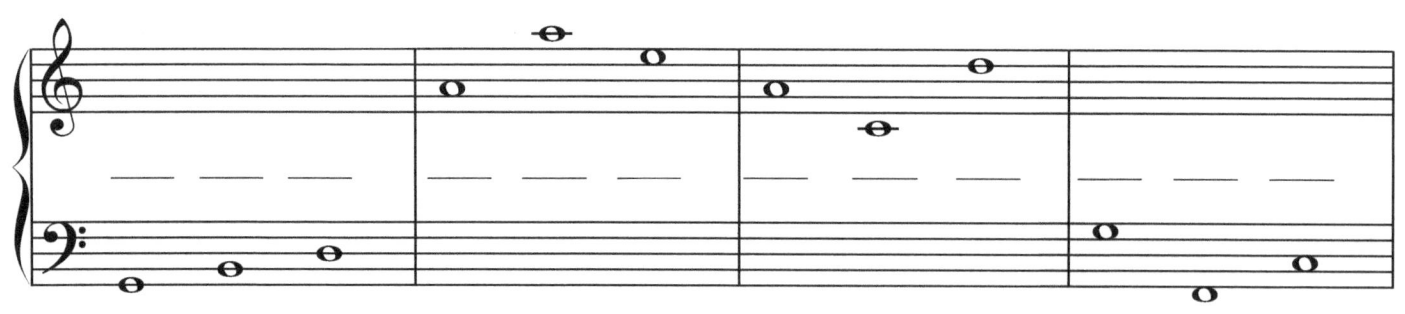
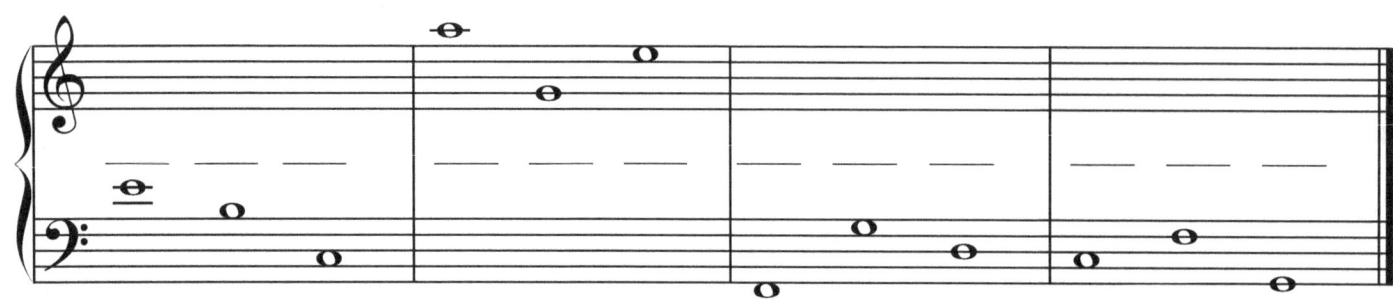

Write the following notes in both the treble and bass clefs of the grand staff.

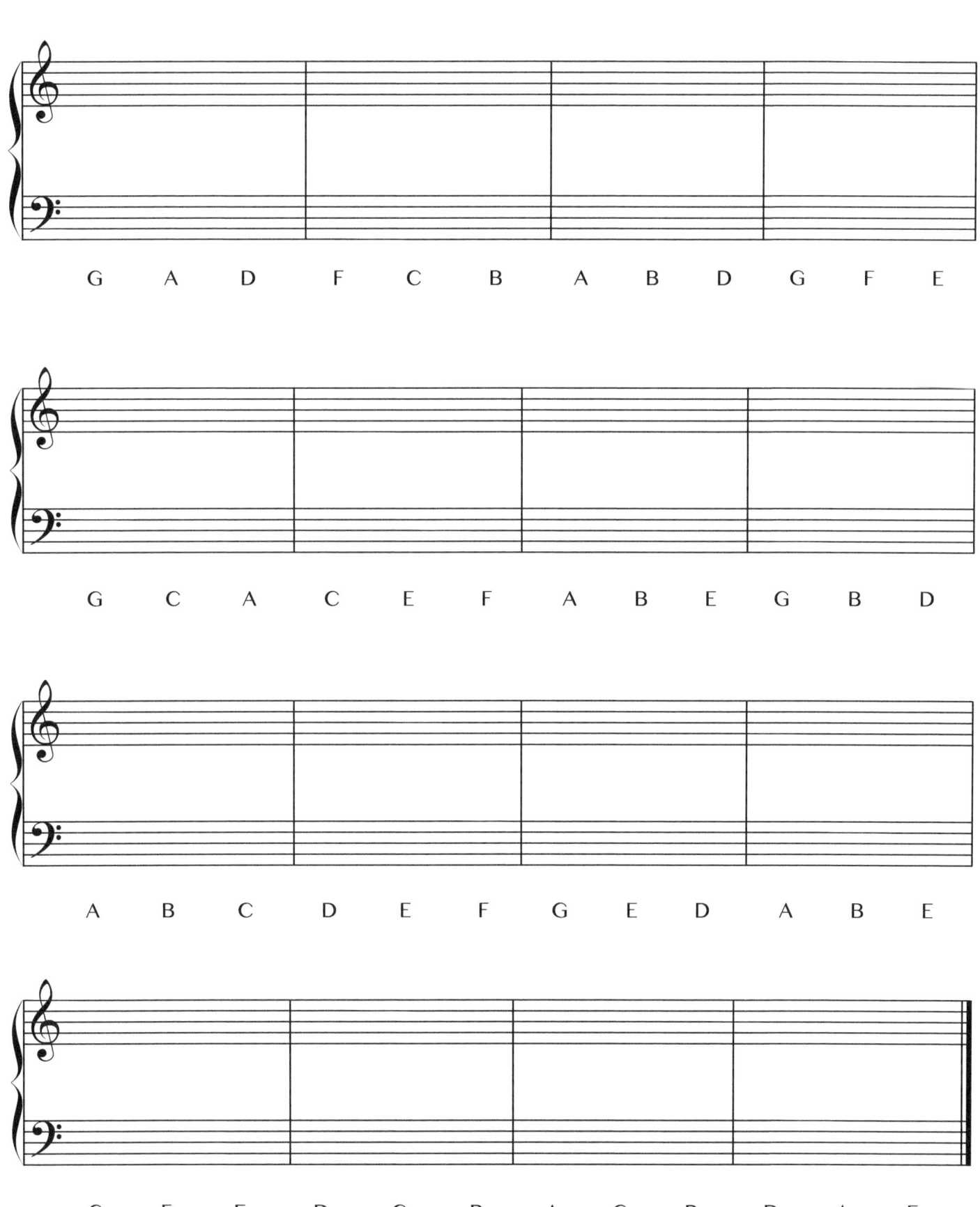

Write the following notes on the grand staff.

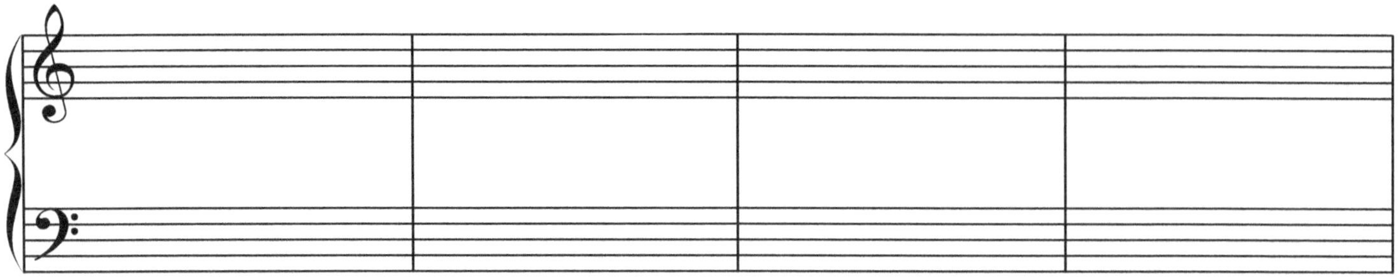

| three different As | three different Bs | three different Cs | three different Ds |

| three different Es | three different Fs | three different Gs | three different As |

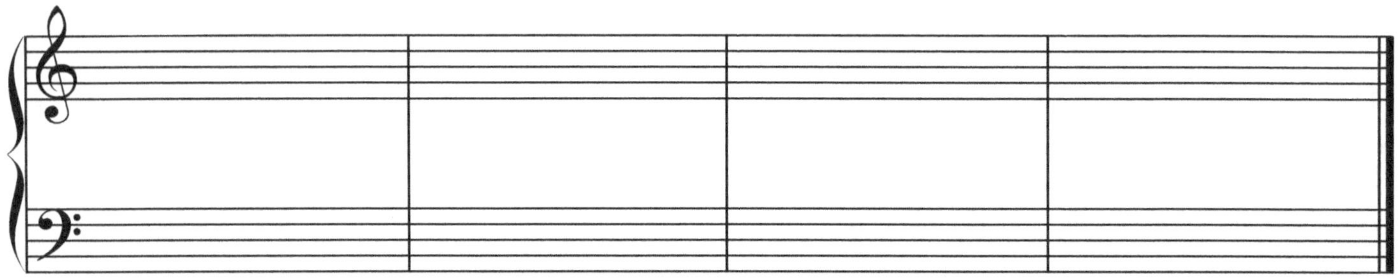

Write the following words using notes in both clefs of the grand staff.

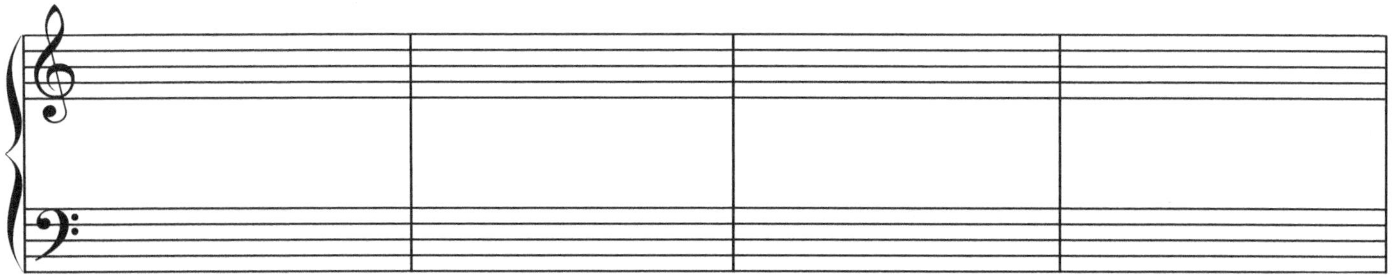

B A B E   A G E D   D E E D   C A G E

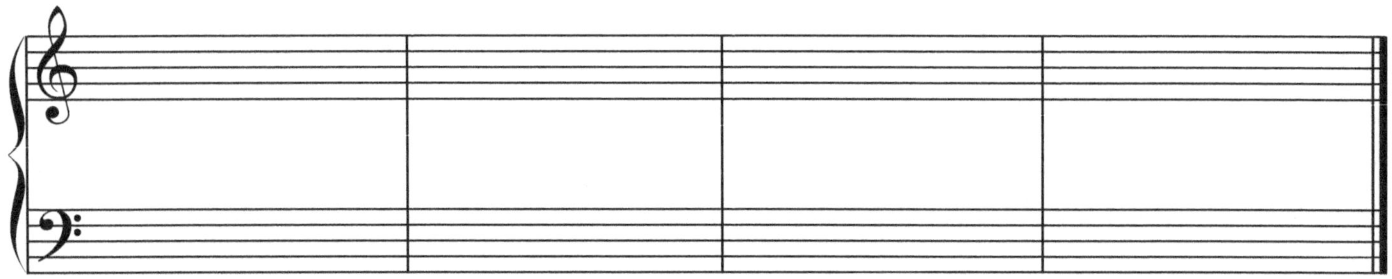

F A C E   G A F F E D   G E   F E E D

Review 3

1. Write all the notes on the grand staff in ascending order. Name each note.

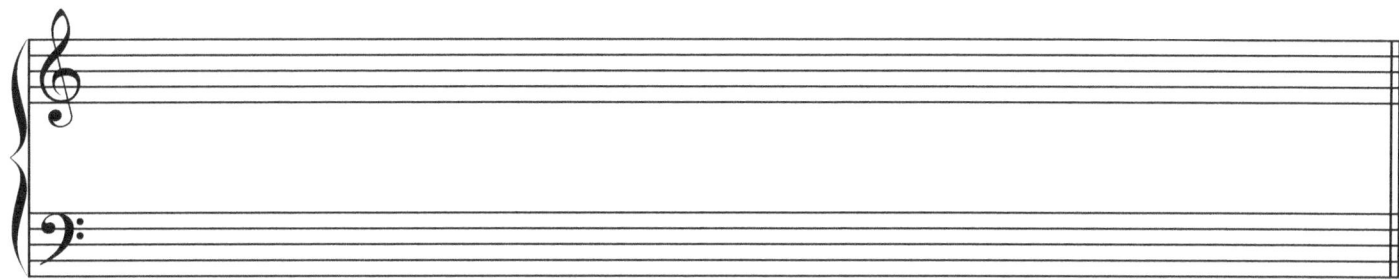

2. Write the following notes on ledger lines above or below the staff.

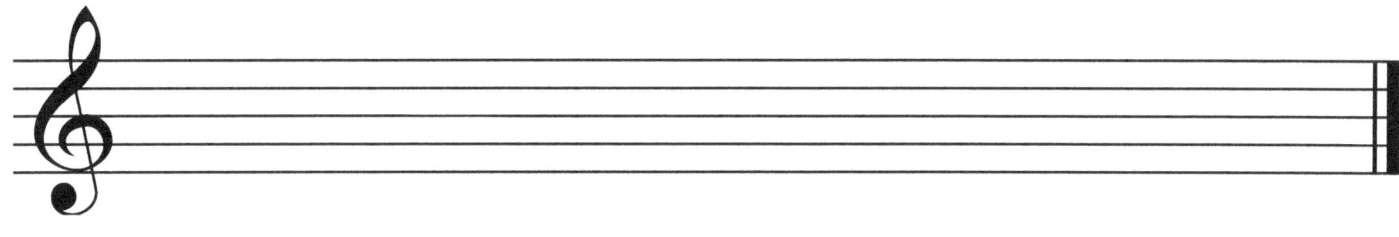

A   C   B   G   B   C   A   C   G   D   A   C   B

3. Write the following notes on ledger lines above or below the staff.

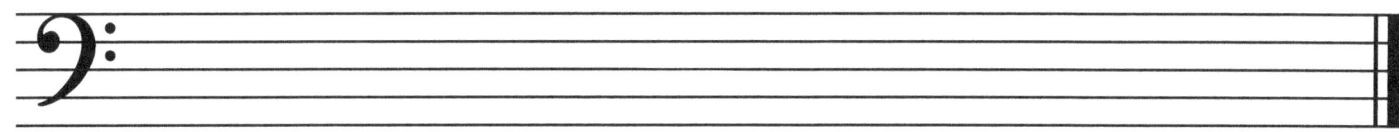

C   D   E   F   B   C   D   E   D   C   E   F   C

4. Name the following notes.

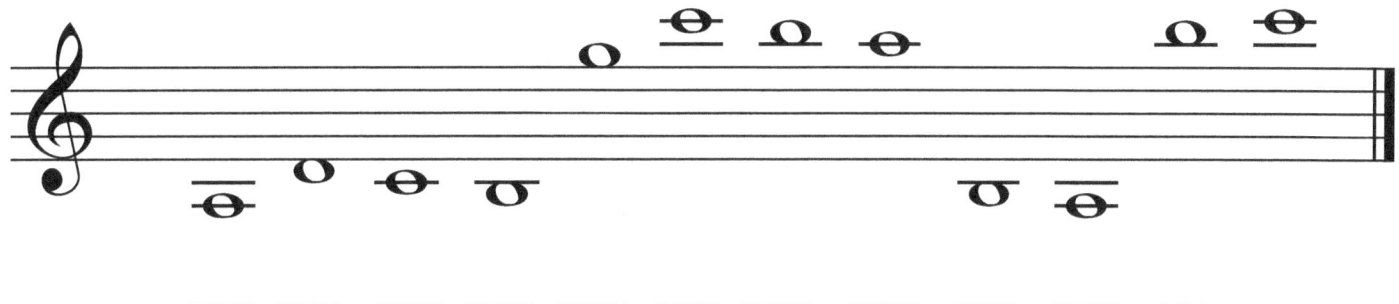

33

5. Name the following notes.

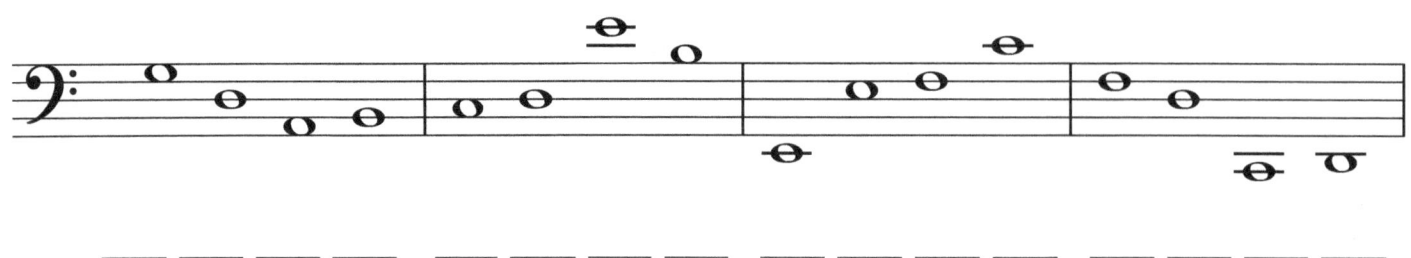

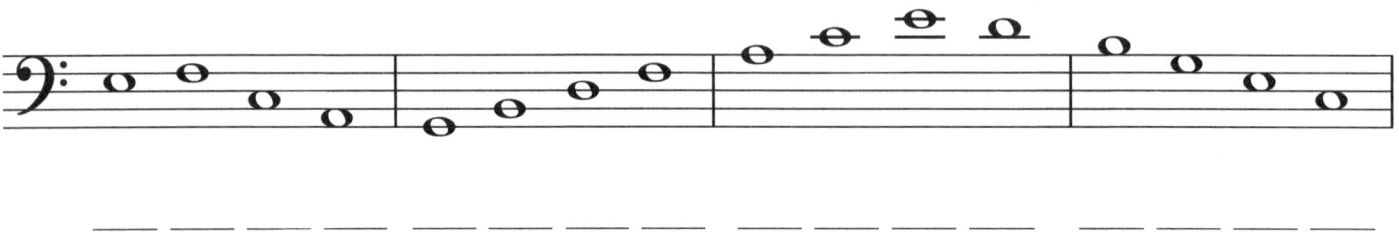

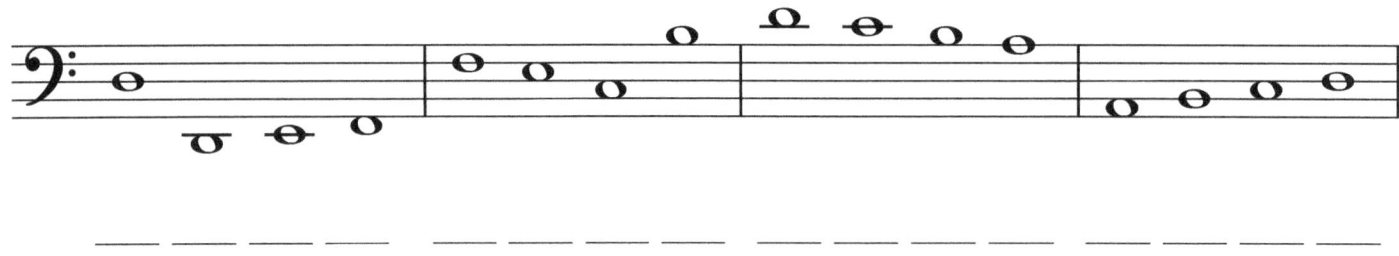

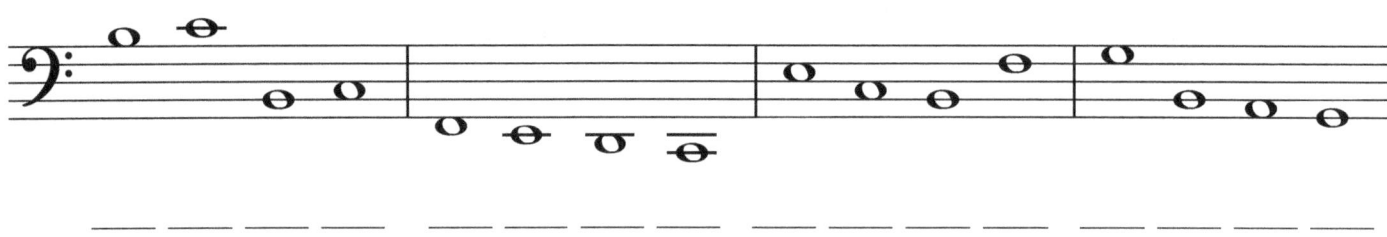

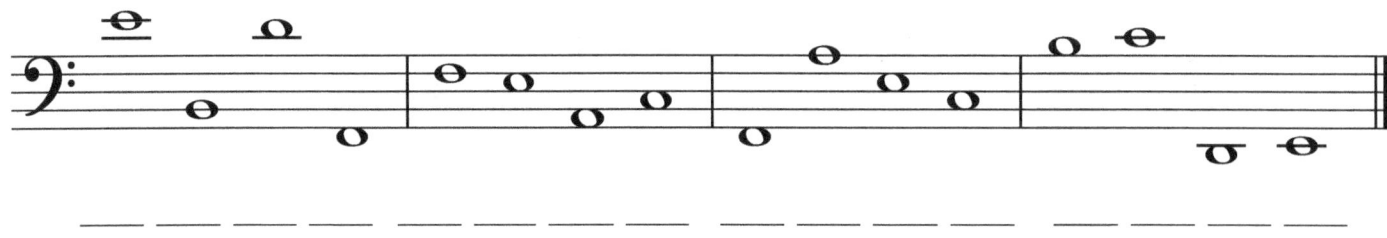

6. Write the following notes.

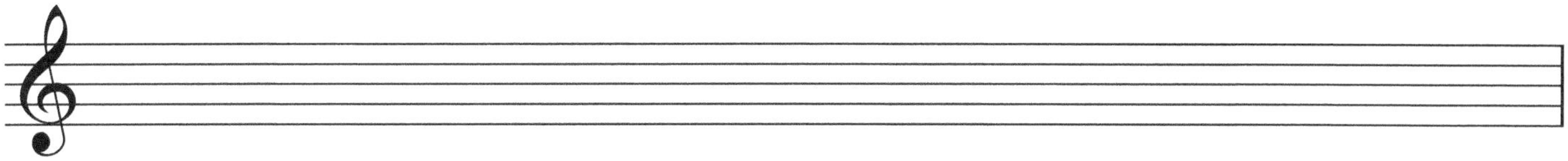

```
G    A    B    F    E    D    C    A


F    E    G    B    A    D    E    B


D    E    F    B    C    G    A    F


A    C    F    G    D    B    E    A


E    F    G    C    A    B    D    E
```

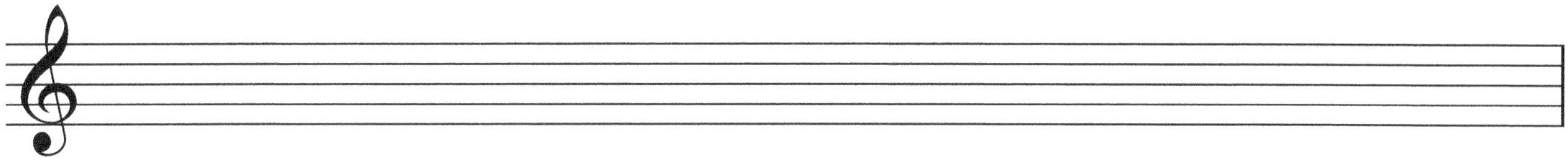

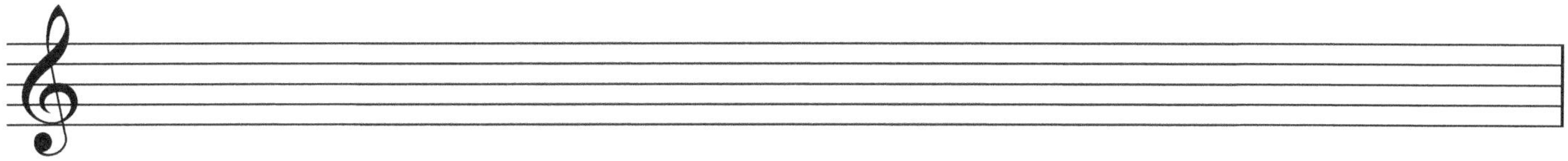

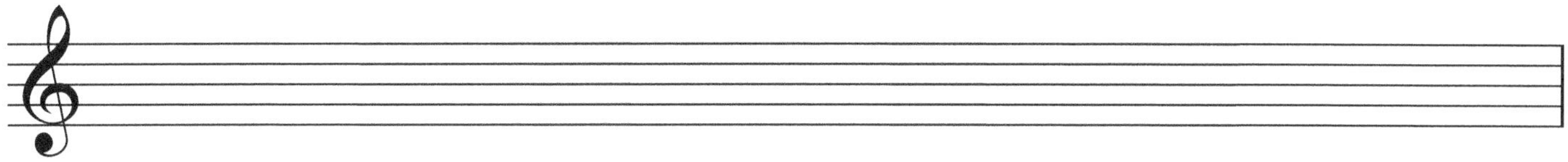

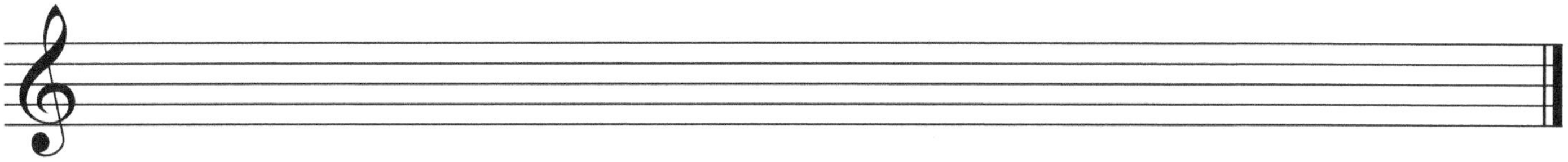

7. Name the following notes.

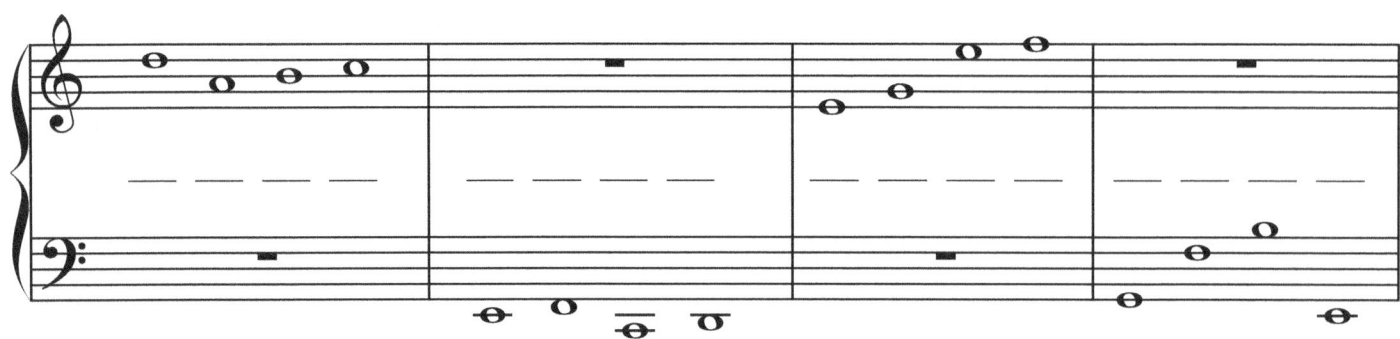
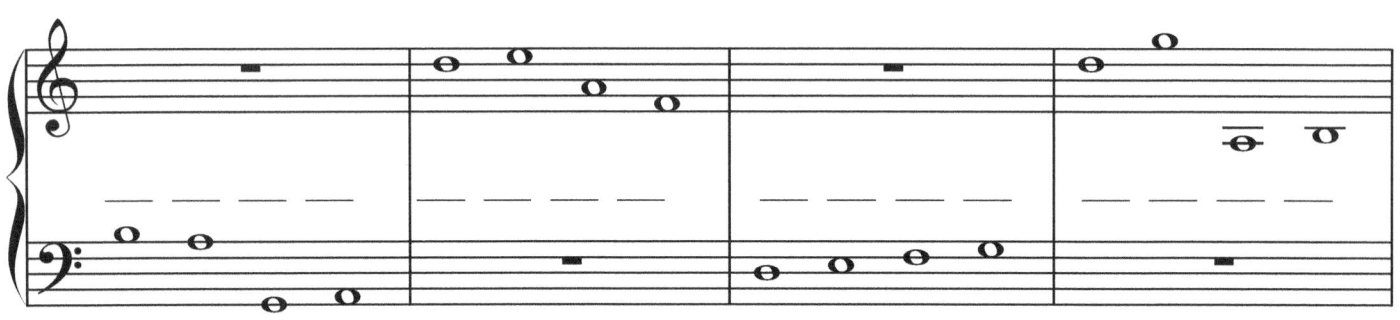
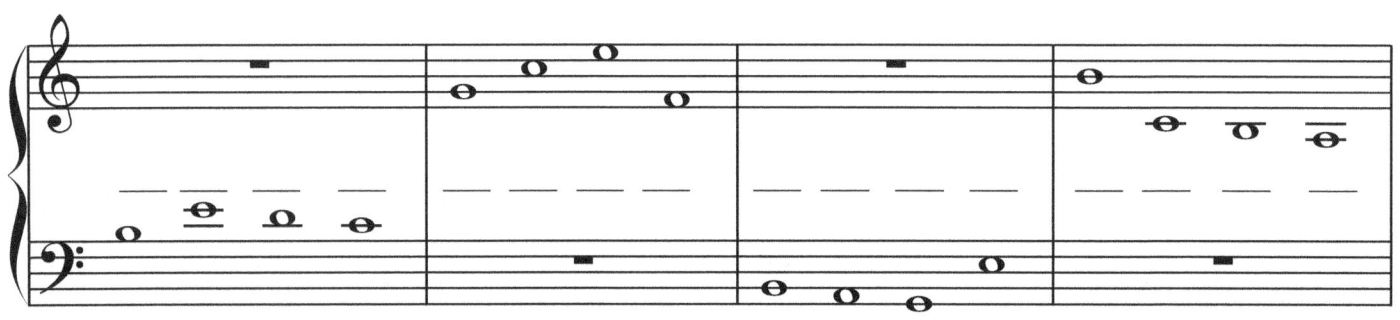
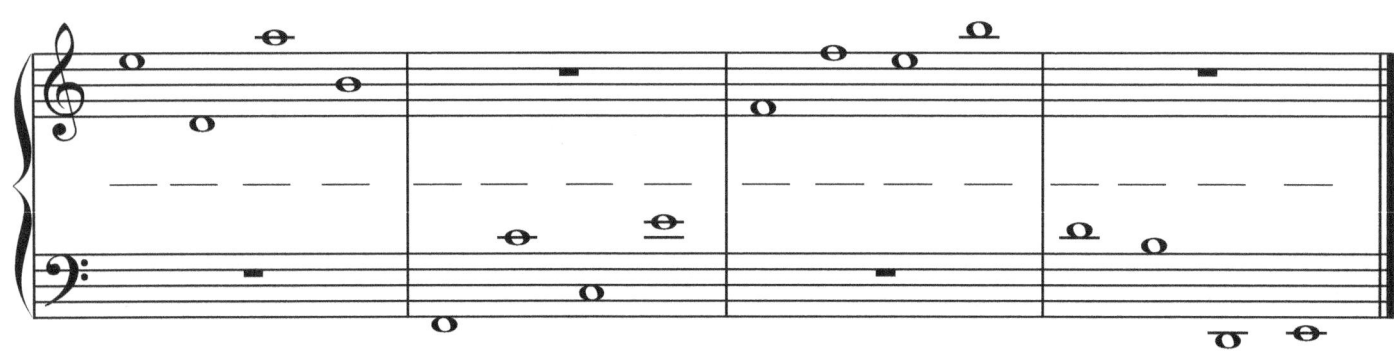